ISBN-: 9781712411803

Dedication

I truly could have dedicated this to a hundred people who have had a positive influence in my life. People that I adore.

I chose to dedicate my first book to my husband Mick.

He picks up the slack of all the household chores that I never get around to, because I haven't grasped the concept that being a stay-at-home parent means I actually need to stay at home sometimes.

Most importantly he picks me up when I'm falling, and I have fallen a lot this year.

The man truly is a saint, because honestly, I can be a right cow sometimes!

I am also very grateful to him for giving me his blessing to write this book. A lot of what happens in our family life is intense and highly personal. We feel being honest about it helps to raise the awareness of what real life for a child with Special Needs, and their family, looks like. This can only be a positive in helping to develop effective support, true acceptance and inclusion.

We don't do soppy declarations of love, but to quote a romantic hero of mine, Edmund Blackadder:

"without you,

life would be like a broken pencil

- pointless."

Acknowledgements

(Basically, the other really important people I didn't dedicate the book to!)

My Wonderful Children

Saoirse, Patrick and Erin, who stayed quiet for enough minutes for Mum to actually finish the book.

I lied to you all, it took more than the "five little minutes" I asked for.

Thank you for being crazy enough to give me so much material to write about!

My Parents

Phil and Val, who without which, I simply wouldn't be here.

Who have saved my ass, more times than is expected of any parent and truly do love me unconditionally, even though I have tested that theory more than once.

My Friends

For always being there, even when I am horrible and for recognising that's when I need you the most.

CoachKarenBrown.com

Who set up my website but made me believe I did it myself, and who has been an excellent life coach to me, even though I don't believe in that stuff.

Aidan Comerford

Whose wonderful book 'Cornflakes for Dinner' got me out of a very deep emotional hole.

Who was polite enough to reply to my fan-mail, gave me the encouragement and confidence to write a little (which quickly became a lot) and who was kind enough to read some of my material and give me feedback.

Paula Kerr

Paula is a Mum of three beautiful boys, Archie, George and Isaac. These three boys suffer from Duchenne Muscular Dystrophy, and Paula runs the charity, Join Our Boys Trust.

This condition is life limiting.

We can all recognise how truly devastating this must be for any parent, and on the days that my life has pushed me to breaking point, feeling I simply cannot dig any deeper and give any more, it is the thought of this inspirational woman that gets me up out of bed.

Because if she can do it, I can.

She is a modern-day gladiator and one of my heroes.

You can find out more about how to support the charity Join Our Boys Trust at the end of this book.

Prologue

I fell off the walking wagon sometime last year.

I even bought a dog to try and get me back on it, but when the dog trainer told me puppies only need a minimal amount of walking in the first year, I took this as a perfect reason to add to my already full arsenal of excuses not to go walking.

However, 2019 saw the Ten-Year Challenge take hold on social media and forced me to take a look at evidence I'd been avoiding.

Whilst I was still rocking the 'yummy mummy' look in 2009, ten years on 2019, was a lot more, '3 weeks passed its sell by date, mummy'. It was a look that no Instagram filter could fix.

As a mum to 3 children, who's waistline since turning 40, was rapidly starting to look more like a coastline, I simply could not ignore that, or poor Heidi (the dog's) pleading eyes anymore. So, I hit the roads of lovely Leitrim, in the West of Ireland, where I live.

I've always liked the sound of my own voice, except on answer phones (obviously), it's a nice way to describe myself, as opposed to saying I never shut up! My head never shuts up either. So, as I pound the lovely green countryside that I'm lucky to have all around me, I often organise my thoughts in written format, as if I were writing a blog or diary. I find it quite therapeutic.

I love language and enjoy listening to articulate people,

who inject humour into their conversation – that's what I want to be when I grow up!

After a particularly long walk with Heidi (9.2km in 91 minutes, 9872 steps – guess who remembered to charge the battery on her fit-bit), I thought maybe it would be good for me to take the thoughts from my head and put them on paper, and that is how my storybook began…

Unlike Leitrim, 'life' doesn't always surround you with beautiful vistas, often times you end up to your eyeballs in muck and shit that threatens to overwhelm you (actually that bit is very much like Leitrim!)

I am married, for 14 years, to Mick and we have three charming children. I have two daughters, Saoirse who is almost 13, Erin who is 6 and a son Patrick, who is 11.

Just like everyone else, life can get a little bit hard sometimes. With each passing year since turning 40 I seem to have gained a stone (14lbs), a bra size and a rapidly increasing set of luggage under my eyes.

An ever-increasing number of situations in recent years, requiring self-administered chocolate therapy, have been a significant factor in my new look.

But one in particular hit hardest.

In 2018, after many turbulent years battling to get support from the abyss, we all like to call 'The System', my son, Patrick, was diagnosed with both ADHD and Autism – boom!

Like buses in a rural town, nothing for five years, and then two come along at once.

I won't say it was a shock exactly, but the Autism part did come as something of a terrifying surprise, maybe something a bit like being told you're expecting triplets.

Manageable but life changing.

As a newly diagnosed 'special needs parent', I spent 2018 successfully completing the 'intense research' stage of my parenting. I passed with flying colours, being awarded the grade: obsessive! Having completed that stage, I transitioned noisily into the 'angry' stage and was feeling generally pissed off with everyone and everything.

I was bordering on the verge of starting to lose friends and/or my sanity, which was hanging on by a thread, and my marriage was also close to taking that big step into 'trouble'. Downsizing my head space, was a top priority, hence why I latched onto the idea of moving some of the thoughts out my head onto paper.

After sharing a few of my written musings with my close friends and family, I was buoyed by the fact that they thought I was quite good at this writing lark.

I do like an audience, so here we are, me having a go at trying to be vaguely amusing, by talking about life's hiccups.

Sometimes they are manageable when you just hold your breath for a few seconds until they pass, other times they turn into an enormous burp and you just have to excuse yourself for a while.

A few scribbles took on a life of their own, and with social media, screaming at me that the end of the decade was nigh, meaning I needed to do something significant, I decided to launch a blog and a book.

So for now, when my kids want me to do a jigsaw with them, or some other such crap, it's a much better excuse to say "I'm writing", than the boring old ones I've been using for years like, "I'm – putting the washing away, in the toilet (yes again!), or I'm running away to join the circus."

I try to find the light in the darker days, with humour and a healthy dose of realism. Navigating my way through the ups and downs of my own 'Ten Year Challenge'.

I hope it will make you smile, make you think, and make you understand why laughter is so important in keeping us functioning day to day.

I believe it is important as water, sunshine and chocolate.

The chapters are short so you can read them whilst sitting on the bus, or to fill the time, when you are waiting for everyone else to finish this month's book club choice.

It's also nothing like an annoying game on X-Box, you don't have to read one chapter to get to the next, just dip in where you feel like it, and enjoy the chaos!

I'd love you to also enjoy my Blog - Bedtime Stories for Mothers and Others', which you can follow on Facebook or Twitter or at www.fayehayden.life.

Finally, I hope you enjoy reading my book, as much as I enjoyed writing it.

It was much cheaper than going to therapy!

Part One - My Family and Other Animals

An introduction to the four most important people in my life and the four legged, furry and feathered creatures that make up our family unit.

Part Two - A Drop Of The Hard Stuff

The last decade has brought challenges I never imagined, for my family and friends. We each have our stories to tell.

This section is dedicated to the very serious things in my life, that have threatened to derail me many times.

Part Three - The Celeriac Crisis

Recently, after starting the low carb Keto Diet, the carb content of the root vegetable celeriac, almost caused me to go 'over the edge; entirely.

To be fair, this celery root, was the last in a long line of challenges that particular day, sent me hurtling to edge, but it is usually the smallest of things that launch us, finally, into oblivion!

Part Four – Going South

We all know how an unexpected and unfair reading on your weighing scales can utterly ruin your day, and let's be honest, turn you into an irritable, slightly rabid, potential serial killer, if anyone dares to mention the way you look or comments on you lunch.

My Anatomy has been ruining my life for years, and it's

about time I had a bit of a laugh at it.

Part Five - Finding a Good Bra

None of us will get through this life without the right support system in place.

This section looks at what helps keep us on the right side of sane, mainly the people, that get us through this crazy little thing called life.

Part One

My Family and Other Animals

The Rock!

The love of my life, no, not chocolate! My husband, Mick.

After a series of non-entity relationships, that always brought heart-ache, nursed with wine, chocolate and a good weepy movie, I thought it might be time to follow my Mum's advice and find myself a "nice boy, not an ass hole".

My Mum had always said that as soon as she saw my Dad, she knew there was something lovely about him. Not a 'love at first sight' kind of way, but just she felt compelled to meet him. On their second date he dropped his false teeth in her lap, clearly not a charmer, but she was hooked.

I moved to Ireland with my job in 2002 and I met Mick on my first night out, and made benign conversation with him in Flynn's Bar. I kept noticing him around work and there was just something about him I was drawn to, an itch I had to scratch.

He was totally oblivious to my pathetic efforts at flirting and six months went by without him barely saying anything to me, except telling me off when I lost my expenses cheque (twice).

Then finally, on Valentine's Day 2003 we had our first kiss, in 'Cartown', the most romantic venue Leitrim has to offer – sticky carpets and all. But like any good, real life romance story, that is where it all began…

My contract in Ireland ended after 2 years, but I

became a local hire as at that stage we were already engaged.

We have been together for 16 years.

It's amazing really that we ever got together at all, what with me being a Brit and all. It wasn't too bad as I was born the right side of the fence, Wales, and chose to become an Irish citizen in 2012, although I still annoy him by saying things like cupboard (closet) and pavement (sidewalk).

I'm not going to bore you with any longwinded Facebook rubbish about how wonderful he is, he just is! He isn't perfect, but he is strong, kind and loving. He cooks, cleans and cares for the children, without being nagged to do so.

He doesn't do conventional romance. On our second anniversary/Valentine's Day – he gave me the free Daniel O'Donnell CD from the paper and a card he'd made himself. I still have the card in my underwear draw, it's precious to me. The Daniel O'Donnell CD, however, went straight in the bin!

He is a very generous and thoughtful man, particularly with his time, and never complains when I need space, or when I'm heading out again to some meeting of one of the many clubs/committees I've joined and I'll never forget the time ordered in Almond M&Ms in from America, when I was pregnant and couldn't eat the peanut ones.

Mick does have one vice – Rugby!!

He is totally obsessed and loves nothing more than

going up to Dublin to watch his beloved Leinster play. Although to be fair, we bought a junior season ticket this year and he always brings one of our gang with him.

They have zero interest in the full 80 minutes and only go for the ice-cream, but it is good quality time.

Mick is the strong silent type and doesn't speak if he doesn't have anything to say. This works well in our relationship as I never stop talking, so I fill in any gaps in the conversation.

But when the rugby is on TV, it all changes, shouting and screaming at the TV. I'd like to consider myself a Scrummy, but in reality, I'm actually just a Rugby Widow who looks more like Paul O'Connell than Posh Spice.

I believe that if we have a strong marriage; it is made so by Mick. He knows me well enough to let me wallow and lose the plot when I need to, but always knows when to pull me back from the brink.

With our life being as it is, we have to function as a team to survive and I feel we do a pretty good job.

Most of the time!

Rule The World

I had always wanted a daughter. I don't know why exactly but I just did.

My wish came true in December 2006, the perfect Christmas present.

I has always planned to call her Eden; (I had read in in a book as a teenager and decided then and there that would be my choice).

But when I was trialling out names at a meeting in work, my colleague piped up "Eden Hayden? You sound like you are yodelling." He was right, so Eden was crossed off the list.

I trawled every baby name book I could find, looked at the credits at the end of every movie and looked up unique celebrity names on-line. But I just couldn't find 'the one'.

Then Mick said, if it was a girl, he would love to call her Saoirse. I liked it, even though I wasn't sure how to spell it!

When the Midwife handed her to me, she said she had never seen a child that looked so much like their father and by God she was right. She was a mini Mick and became known as Mick in a dress.

I loved her the second I saw her, but I came to learn a few weeks later, that the consuming love you feel for your children doesn't always happen the very second you see them.

I was changing her nappy, when she was close to a month old, and I burst into tears, because I was just so happy and overwhelmed to be a Mum.

I was hooked, being utterly besotted with my baby girl

and could never be without her.

Her first smile was on January 24th 2007.

I remember the date because it is my birthday. It is the best birthday present I know I will ever get. (Some Tiffany diamond earrings would make a close second Mick, if you are reading this 😊)

When she was a baby, I used to dance around the kitchen with her and my favourite song was 'Rule The World' by Take That.

I would sing it loudly and completely out of tune and she loved it.

I don't have a favourite child, I love them all differently, but the same. I know that doesn't make sense but it's true.

There are times when I have felt closer to each of my children, but the love is always equal. But with Saoirse, she has the distinction that, I have loved her the longest.

Having recently turned 13 and now in Secondary School, I can't believe where the years have gone. She told me just before Christmas last year, that she "knew" the big secret.

I pretended not to know what she was talking about, but she was insistent that she wasn't a little girl anymore and I wasn't allowed to keep up the pretence any longer. She warned me not to cry!

I wasn't actually as upset as I thought I would be by her revelation.

It was a big indicator that she was growing up and hurtling towards womanhood a lot quicker than I would like, but our relationship was changing too.

I strongly believe in being a parent, before being a friend to our children, but we all hope to have a good and happy relationship with our kids.

I have always enjoyed being in Saoirse's company, just nowadays it's not because of the cute things she says but because of the intelligent things she says.

She has always been a big reader, to the point that we have to remind her that it isn't actually safe to walk through the school carpark reading a book and we would like her to stop doing it!

Lately, Saoirse has taken to reading books about strong, impressive women in history and I believe she is becoming a strong, impressive young women too: she respects people for who they are, she makes time for everyone and is a great sister to both of her siblings.

Saoirse is animal mad and wants to run her own animal rescue when she grows up. Our home is filled will animals of all shapes and sizes, many of them have been freed from unpleasant lives, including our four battery hens, who she lovingly nursed back to full health, spending her own pocket money buying them chicken vitamins.

Saoirse is a good person. Everyone who meets her tells me how impressed by her they are.

I am so proud to have a daughter who thinks for herself, who doesn't judge people and makes a positive difference to the world.

Saoirse may never rule the world like the song says, but she has certainly changed mine, forever.

A Special Package

My son Patrick arrived three days early.

He's been very thoughtful since day 1, as he was actually due the day of Mick's brother's wedding and not wanting to hog the limelight, he decided 3 days was the perfect space between a new baby and a wedding.

When in labour with Patrick, my epidural didn't work and being a total drama queen who wants an anaesthetic for a broken nail, I told the Midwife I thought I would need to have a C-section. She just laughed at me and handed me the gas mask.

Luckily, he didn't hang around and all 9lb 8oz of him appeared on a rainy Wednesday in October 2008.

My life would change for ever, just not in a way I ever expected.

He was the biggest of my three babies and everyone kept telling me how huge he was. I didn't get it, I thought he was teeny.

That was until I saw him beside other newborns, then I realised he looked like he could have eaten one them for a snack.

Despite regularly suffering reflux akin to a volcanic eruption, he grew rapidly and soon became a little chunky monkey.

I used to love his fat thighs and would blow raspberries on them calling them his little squishers. He would squeal with delight and to this day is ridiculously ticklish.

Just like with Saoirse, my intense love of him wasn't immediate - it isn't like the movies! It was a slower burner, but by the time he was 4 weeks old, I was totally smitten.

I have always said that this little man carries my heart around in his pocket. He had a smile that would light a town and a glint in his eye that perfectly complimented his sense of mischief.

Saoirse couldn't say Patrick and for ages he was known as 'Package'. Sadly, an over-zealous carer in the creche decided to teach Saoirse the correct way to say his name. I was gutted when she refused to call him Package anymore. Nowadays, he goes by 'Dude'.

Patrick has always been the child that has caused me the greatest level of worry.

Along with his reflux, he had glue ear and a shocking dose of chicken pox all before his first birthday.

This decade began terribly for Patrick, at just fifteen months old, he contracted the Rota Virus, due to por quality drinking water following an incident with frozen pipes.

We became alerted to it when he suffered a terrible seizure that caused him to stop breathing.

Mick was changing his nappy and he screamed for me to call an ambulance.

This is the one and only time I have ever heard panic in Mick's voice.

Mick breathed for him and eventually he vomited and started to breathe again.

For about two minutes that day I thought we had lost him, it remains, the worst day of my life.

After 2 more seizures, a week in hospital, an MRI, a lumber puncture, litres of blood being taken and a pharmacy full of anti-viral and anti-biotic drugs being pumped into his tiny body, he was allowed home.

All of the drugs meant he was now very healthy and super energetic.

A week in the hospital with a toddler with, at that time un-diagnosed ADHD, was like trying to wrestle an octopus in a bathtub, so getting home brought true joy, and a decent night's sleep.

He was a little live wire and from an early age and has been into absolutely everything. As a toddler he used to crawl around the floor eating mud out of plant pots. The day of Saoirse's 5th birthday party, I was preparing lots of the 'healthy yet fun' food (who knew what you could do with beetroot!), intent on impressing my newly acquired and very shiny, school gate mummy friends. Patrick, who was 3, said to me "here you go mummy" I turned around and he handed me my oven door!!

WTF!!??

He was in super power mode obviously, and that was before I'd even given him the sneaky sugar filled Haribo I had tucked away.

Then, there was what he did to my car when he was 4!

After a very big night out the night before, I was feeling a little fragile. I'm not a big drinker normally, but this was one of those nights that had run away with me.

Mick had popped out, and Saoirse and Patrick had been playing in the front garden, whilst I left the front door open listening to them, lying very still on the couch to reduce my nausea.

Saoirse ran into the house to tell me Patrick had broken the car.

I dragged myself out to see what had happened with his toy car, only to realise it wasn't his car, but mine!

In an effort to clean it for me, Patrick had taken the yard brush into the back seat and had shattered the back window. Amazingly it was still intact!

I gently lifted him out of the car and as I shut the door the glass went everywhere, fortunately he was fine and just beamed at me, feeling proud of his cleaning skills!

When he is calm, Patrick is a gentle giant.

He is kind, loving and engaging and I just love to get cuddles from him, he gives great ones. Like any typical child of his age he loves rugby, PS4 and nerf guns, He will tell you in animated detail about all of the things he loves: dinosaurs, sharks, and each of the emergency services, especially the Police.

In 2018, after 4 years of battling the Health Service to pay attention to us telling them, that something was wrong, Patrick was diagnosed with ADHD and Autism. Whilst we focus as much as we can on a strength-based approach with Patrick, and he has so many wonderful qualities, the thing that makes me so sad about Patrick's diagnosis, is that often it robs us of this beautiful boy.

He has virtually no emotional regulation ability and suffers from extreme anxiety. The slightest thing can set him into a rage as a way to communicate how he is feeling.

Patrick's special needs, do not excuse his behaviour, but they do explain it.

I never allow Patrick to simply hurt people and not deal with it. I aim to help people understand the root of this aggressive behaviour. It is a form of communication for some people that struggle to communicate any other way. It is often the only way he can tell me the level of anguish and even pain he is experiencing.

Underneath this behaviour, is a loving, caring, wonderful child, who despite his challenges, I love to infinity and beyond.

A World Filled With Joy

The summer of 2013, my life was complete.

I had two beautiful children already and after two miscarriages my third child arrived, very quickly at Mullingar General Hospital, Westmeath.

I had kept Mick, and a bus full of school children entertained by doing my 'Lions Breath' yoga breathing in the car on the trip to the hospital. I didn't care what I looked like, hilarious apparently! It kept me going for the hour-long journey.

Being the wuss that I am, I cried for an epidural even though the Midwife told me the baby might arrive before the anaesthetist. Erin arrived very quickly, giving us all a fright when she came out looking a bit like Violet Beauregard – deep purple!

She was fine, thankfully! The Midwife handed her to me and it was love at first sight. As I've said, with my first two children, the overwhelming love came after a few weeks but with Erin it was instantaneous. Maybe because I knew that love already with Saoirse and Patrick or maybe because she born after loss, but I was immediately hooked. With now three, healthy children I felt a nice sense of smug contentment.

Erin is what you would call in Ireland; 'A flyer'. She was always ahead of the game and we joked she has been here before. She walked at eleven months, said her first word "Saoirse" or "Sisa" a week later.

Erin is the hungriest child I have ever met; she literally

never stops eating and her main source of distress is if she ever feels that is going to miss out on food someone else might be getting. She was the tallest junior infant I have ever seen and is head and shoulders above anyone her age in group photos. Despite being six, she wears age 10-11 clothes and has size 2 feet.

A big body needs a big personality to fill it and that is our Erin, or Erie Berry as we like to call her.

She is wild and free and does her own thing. If you tell her what to do then she always has a perfectly logical and plausible reason about why she shouldn't do it. It's very difficult to argue with her as she really is always right and the funny little faces she pulls when explaining herself always make it difficult to keep a straight face myself.

I have always thought we mis-named Erin and should have called her Joy.

She is the happiest child, I've ever met. She has struggled a lot this year, dealing with the very big emotions, the challenges her brother's difficult behaviour creates. Being assessed for Autism herself this summer, when her meltdowns and anxiety became severe and overwhelming for us all. This brought a lot of big emotions for Mick and particularly me too. We have been told, that it is unlikely she is Autistic, but the Psychologists do see a lot of challenges for her and will be monitoring how she copes. Through intensive play therapy to help her along and a very special new class teacher, she has thankfully regained her magic and sparkle and my Joy is very welcome back.

Erin is loud, and giddy and always a whirlwind, spinning and dancing into every room, singing at the top her voice to her karaoke machine – Santa, what were you thinking?! She just loves make believe and after watching Re-runs of The Great British Bake Off, with her big sister, they pretend to be Mary and Paul dishing out a critique of every dinner I make, checking to make sure there is "no soggy bottom!"

I'm enjoying her whilst I can because I have no doubt this little wonder woman will be off to live somewhere exciting like New York or Paris the first chance she gets or maybe it'll be Jupiter, because she is out of this world!

The Beast From The East

Ireland has always been obsessed with the weather. It as much a staple of our daily conversations as tea is to our breakfast.

In recent times, we have gotten on first name terms with our storms, "Oh I hear Deirdre's on her way, and she's in shocking bad form" could be a conversation you would in the pensions queue at the local post office and not know if it refers to an impending hurricane, or a long-lost cousin returning from Dublin.

Probably, the worst weather event of recent years, that lived up to the exciting weather predictions, was in 2018 with the arrival of the 'Beast from the East', which saw snow in March. Here in Leitrim, more specifically our house, we got our own Beast from the East, but it arrived in July not March 2018. Her name was Heidi!

Early in 2018 our two longest serving family pets died. Our beloved dogs, Rhea and Henke died within two months of each other. Given that I had been complaining about them peeing on the floor for the past year (Rhea was sixteen to be fair), I was surprised to realise, that I actually really missed having them around. So, when Saoirse saw an advert in a local shop for Labrador puppies, I managed to convince (i.e. whinge long enough) my husband that we 'needed' another dog.

As Patrick is Autistic, in my mind he simply had to have a companion dog in case he struggles to make friends as he gets older. I envisaged they would be inseparable, the dog would sleep in his room and put in an Oscar worthy performance as his best friend, just like in all the best dog companion movies.

As the dog was going to be Patrick's, he got to choose the breed.

Patrick is obsessed with all things Police, so it had to be a German Shepherd. He got no arguments from us as Rhea was half German Shepherd and we were all still grieving her loss. We set about sourcing German Shepherd puppies in an ethical way (Done Deal obviously). Me being me, we had to have it within a week, as I don't do this 'waiting' lark. We found a litter of little beauties over in Dublin (Kennel Club Approved). She was tiny and adorable. We whittled down our shortlist of German names, and with some big sisterly 'encouragement', Patrick settled on Heidi. And so, the love affair with our dog began - erm NO – she's an absolute lunatic that has added to my stress levels exponentially and I spend most of my time cursing the day we got her.

An annoying habit she had as a puppy, was to eat her own poo and anyone else's she came across - the chicken's, other dogs', she really wasn't fussy. Fortunately, I don't see her doing it often anymore, but I have observed a distinct lack of poo in our garden when I do my weekly poo patrol. It has to go somewhere, so I'm guessing she's still at it. This is the reason why you should never let dogs lick you. EVER!!

She grew very quickly. Don't get me wrong, I knew she would be big, but if anyone remembers the TV programme 'V' from the 80s, she grew like the alien children in that, from 0 to 100 in less than a second.

We have chickens and duck, who I am proud to say are free range and have the free run of our back garden/mud-pit.

We put up a fence between the back and the front of the house, but Heidi kept finding a way through and we then had to catch her – can you recognise the irony of running around like a headless chicken trying to prevent a chicken becoming headless!

To be fair though, she left Johnny Sexton, the duck, alone. I don't blame her on that one, he's a vicious little fecker who would gladly peck your eyes out!

As she's grown bigger her jumping up at people has gotten to be a real problem. It's not quite so bad when she does it to us. But when she starts doing it to visitors it can be a serious issue. One of our neighbour's children often comes to play and one day Heidi jumped up and grabbed her by the pigtail. Luckily our neighbour has four kids, of which this child is the youngest, so she doesn't freak out easily, but there are limits to everyone's patience.

Heidi is indiscriminate when it comes to who she'll knock over, and recently floored my Mother-in-law's friend, who is pushing 80.

This lady uses bad language befitting of an inner-city Dublin matriarch, even though she's from Ballinteer, a suburb beside Dundrum just not as posh. Let's just say that, as she was toppled to the ground by our adorable puppy there were a few choice F's, B's and C's coming out of her mouth.

Heidi likes to jump up at the half door that separates her room and the kitchen. At first it was cute like a baby peeking over his cot when he learns to stand. Now I'm worried she'll go over, or possibly even through, the bloody door!

She is also ridiculously noisy.

Many people with Autism will engage in self-stimulatory behaviour, it's known as 'stimming'. You may often see an Autistic person rocking back and forth or flapping their hands wildly. As a neuro-typical person, we must overcome our urge to stop them doing this, just because it seems 'weird' to us. It is vital the person be allowed to stim, as it helps to keep them calm and regulate their emotions in challenging situations.

Patrick's stim of choice, is to screech, very loudly.

He does it a lot before and straight after school to help him cope and sometimes if he's surrounded by too many people.

Heidi screeches too.

She's not Autistic, just a pain in the arse.

She likes to share her very loud high-pitched bark with us all if she thinks we aren't paying her enough attention, which is most of the time.

On the plus side, when everyone else has left the house and it's just me and Heidi I do respond to her with a loud screech myself, something along the lines of "shut the fuck up Heidi".

It's great for releasing my own daily tensions.

Another plus is that Heidi is my walking buddy.

Again, like a small baby it takes at least ten minutes to get her out of the house by the time I've collected up all of her paraphernalia - poo bags, treats for rewarding good behaviour, an iron bar for dealing with bad behaviour (don't call the ISPCA, I'm joking).

We've given up on a muzzle for the time being, as three quarters of the walk wearing one, consisted of me trying to drag her along the lane as tries to get the stupid thing off, by doing forward rolls like a drunken man on his way home from a serious session. If I had a spare hand to make a video of her doing this, I'd make a bloody fortune on YouTube!

I have to wrestle her into her dog harness every day.

It's some fancy new thing that Mick got and looks like one of those mad stringy swimsuits that WAGs wear on their many sun holidays.

The harness is great when it works, but if you put it on the wrong way, which I often do, then the poor dog ends up walking along looking like a dressage horse on speed for the whole trip.

Taking her on a walk does make me a bit nostalgic as she loves splashing in muddy puddles, just like my kids did in their Peppa Pig phase, and she is very cute when she chases leaves, thinking she can fly.

I also enjoy throwing things around the garden for her

to catch: sticks, a ball, dynamite!

We have quite a big garden so she gets a good run.

I usually do this in the mornings, so I'm out there in my foxy dressing gown (it's not silky and sexy, it's just actually designed to look like a fox), sometimes bra, sometimes not and my Fit-Flops.

The only problem is, that our garden is positioned right on a very bad bend on the lane we live on, so people generally slow down when they come up to it, meaning my neighbours often get to see me in all my resplendent morning glory. My husband must be so proud! I can't just leave her alone in the garden, as she can open doors and will come in forlornly looking for a someone to play with.

In the evenings, Heidi jumps up on the sofa and stretches out between Mick and I, surveying her domain whilst snuggling in for a cuddle. My heart melts a little bit when she's like that, and I do look at her and think I can put up with all her faults, because, as a L'Oréal advert would tell me – she's worth it (I hope!)

Meadow Therapy

A while ago, my friend sent me a text to say she had just seen something very unexpected.

Little green men?

The Sam Maguire Cup in Leitrim?

No, it was me in gym bunny gear, yes that is unusual, but not what she meant.

I was throwing a bale of hay over a gate and then climbing over the gate and dragging the hay though a field.

I'm not a city girl. I grew up in a small industrial town in North Wales. I lived on the outskirts of the town in a cul-de-sac that was adjacent to miles and miles of fields. I've always enjoyed country walks and fresh air, but I'm definitely not the farming type. I'd me more comfortable in Jimmy Choos than Hunter wellies, not that I can afford either!

So, the sight of me wrestling with a hay bale on a cold Leitrim morning is pretty unexpected.

As usual, I was late getting my daughter to school, so I was off to do her morning job of feeding her animals.

You've already met Heidi but now it's time to introduce the three biggest members of our animal family. Meadow and Hughie the horses and Shadow the donkey.

My husband Mick doesn't remember learning to ride as he was so young when he did. He was always around horses growing up and with his horse Jono, he regularly went up against his older brother Pat (and Ringo) in show jumping competitions every week. It was a such a huge part of his life.

Mick's Dad died when Mick was only 13 after as short battle with cancer. As well as the devastating blow of losing his beloved Dad, with eight mouths between the ages on 2-15 to feed, there was simply no way to keep the horses. This was no doubt another huge loss in his life. He didn't complain or make a fuss, because he's the kind of person accepts what happens in life and gets on with. This is a trait that has been so very important in our recent lives.

By the age of four Saoirse was showing a huge interest in animals and after having her first ride and first fall on my friend's pony, we decided to start her at the Hayden's the local stables (no relation). She was a natural and barring a problem with never holding her reigns tight enough at the start she flew along.

By the age of eight she had convinced us to let her spend her Saturdays at the stables helping out. Since then, that is exactly where she has spent every Saturday and most of her summer holidays. She has made brilliant friends and works very hard when there, teaching her discipline and a strong work ethic. Also, it's a very cheap summer camp, as all she needs is a fiver a week for the tuck shop.

Saoirse's biggest dream has always been to have her own horse.

Last year, when working out our finances we decided we could stretch to a horse of her own. I know a few people think having a horse means you have loads of money but trust me we really don't.

When you have a horse, you are either super rich or constantly skint, we are the latter.

Someone was on our side when we started horse shopping, as I was scrolling through the ads a new one appeared, for a horse that, on paper, was perfect and she was half our budget. My Dad always taught me that if something seems too good to be true, then it probably is. But with this one, I had to try.

The next day, with Saoirse's super helpful and dedicated riding instructor in tow, we travelled over to Roscommon to view 'Lady'.

My goodness, she is a lady, a beautiful dapple-grey mare. Aileen, the girl selling her had been training her for years and had grown too big for her. She was a lovely girl who bred and trained horses, each of whom she felt a strong connection too. She just wanted Lady to go to a good home where she would be loved and cared for. The deal was struck.

After years of challenging times in our family, where Saoirse has never complained and had done her absolute best to look after her brother and sister, and at times me, it meant the absolute world to us to make her dream a reality. We also consider it to be a very important part of managing her mental health. Being able to ride is a great outlet for Saoirse to escape and blow off steam when things get hard at home. Particularly as her teenage years are approaching and she wants to escape us all.

Saoirse decided to change the horse's name from My Lady Black Jack to My Lady Meadow Brooke. Meadow Brook is the name of the stables Mick's Dad ran and where his and Pat's ponies lived. This was the perfect name to remember Mick's Dad and make a special connection.

To us she is just Meadow.

She's a temperamental, fiery bugger at times, just like her owner Saoirse – they are a perfect match.

To keep Meadow company we acquired a donkey, Shadow. He belonged to a lovely local farmer who when I asked if I could buy him said No, but I could have him. He was very kind and even paid to get his hooves clipped and him castrated before he gave him to us.

I don't think Shadow considered being castrated to be very kind. But we did!

One day, Shadow the donkey escaped over a hedge and onto the main road for a little run around, when Meadow was at the riding stables, we decided he needed company when Meadow was gone. So, we adopted Hughie from the local horse rescue centre and now they are an inseparable gang.

They have come with an added stress relieving benefit for me. There is a lot of work that goes into having a horse, so we all muck in and muck out.

I went to help Saoirse clear muck from the field recently, we only have one rake, so Saoirse told me to use my foot!

What?

So, embracing country life and keen to try out my new heavy-duty wellies, I thought, that the hell and started kicking it out around with my foot.

That is how I discovered my alternative therapy!

It is so damn satisfying to quite literally kick the 'shit' out of something.

I know it may sound aggressive, but it's literally hurting no one and giving my thighs a good workout. Although I would be lying if I said I don't often imagine the head of our current inept Health Minister, Simon Harris' perched on the top of one of the piles of dung. I always give it an extra hard kick if he is there, I'm not sure Peppa Pig would agree that is how wellies should be used!

I would like to confirm, that I always give my wellies a really good wash at the hose before leaving the field.

Johnny Sexton And The Rest Of The Team

I used to love watching child behaviour programmes Super Nanny and Dr Tanya Byron the child psychologist on TV.

I once saw Dr Tanya speak on a video conference, and I loved her honesty and realistic approach to parenting.

She told a story of how her friend pretended, Dr Tanya's kids were her own, when they were acting out in a shopping centre and everyone was staring judgmentally, as Dr Tanya should apparently have better behaved kids.

She very truthfully told of how, she felt guilty about it, but not so guilty she didn't sneak off to Starbucks for a Latte and leave her friend to it. That's the kind of friends you want!

These programmes often suggested time to think, and the concept of 'Time Out' began common practice. I've used it with my own children to limited effect.

It did however work really well with Johnny Sexton, our duck!

Yes, you did read that right.

We decided we would have a go at keeping chickens 3 years ago.

After the first three got savaged by the scourge of the Irish countryside, a pine marten, we took a little break but eventually got 3 more, who I am glad to say, all bar the ill-fated, Rex, are all still alive today.

We have added to our little gang of common reds, with Blanket, a beautiful bantam hen, who as chickens go, is a bit of a supermodel.

Last year we decided to also get a duck.

He started out just like the cute little yellow fluffy ones you see in children's books, but he quickly grew, and grew and grew some more.

He grew so much we weren't actually sure if we'd bought a goose by mistake.

But no, he's a pekin duck – just like Donald and Daisy.

We bought him with a chick, Blueberry, at the same time and they are inseparable. At first, I don't think he realised himself, he was a duck being surrounded by chickens. He never went into the pond, until one day he fell in and realised he loved it. He still doesn't seem to realise he's different to the chickens and regularly splashes them with his water as if they are missing out on all the fun.

Last Year, I saw an appeal on Facebook to rescue former battery hens that were in an awful state. I hate battery farming, so we decided to give 2 a home, in the end we took 4.

I thought this would be a great opportunity for Saoirse to see the real side of dealing with rescuing animals.

It's not all cute puppies and kittens, but sadly more likely to be mistreated animals at death's door that need a lot of time and effort to be nursed back to health.

She rose to the challenge and they are now healthy

and thriving.

We slowly integrated 'The Lovely Ladies' as we called them, in with the rest of the other chickens and all went well.

Johnny Sexton, however, was a different story.

He was very territorial and would chase them around the garden pecking at them. He is big, with a strong beak so he can land a mighty blow if he gets close.

In the end we had to make the decision he needed 'time out'. He was moved to an old dog pen, still in the garden so he could see the other chickens. Apparently, ducks are very sensitive and can get depressed if left on their own.

Whilst we didn't want him to hurt the chickens, we didn't want this segregation to damage his mental health either!

After about a month, and a few challenging encounters, he seemed to settle and now they all live happily ever after.

They are fully free range and regularly go off on little adventures in the field beside ours, but they are always back by bedtime.

To complete the chaos, we also have 2 musk turtles, Ruby and Riley.

Saoirse wrote a 50-page project on the care of turtles, to convince us to let her get them and paid for them and their tank with her Communion money.

They are a lifetime commitment and will probably

outlive us. We have a ten-year plan of where they will move to the shed in our garden, when they outgrow the tank.

Finally, there is Arthur the rabbit, who we adopted last year. We were told he was blind, and no one would take him. Being a Disabilities Advocate, I couldn't leave him behind. Turns out he's not blind after all, but he's not going back.

The animals are a big part of our lives, Saoirse's in particular.

They add A LOT of extra stress to my life, but I'm obviously a glutton for punishment and a sucker for a sob story. We really have reached the limit now, although Saoirse has asked for a pig for her birthday.

I wonder if I could convince Mick?!?!?!?

Part Two

A Drop Of The Hard Stuff

When I Grow Up...

I was 25, when I attended the funeral of a friend for the first time.

It was a sobering experience.

Rosaria Merola, a gorgeous girl I was at secondary school with, was killed in a car-crash.

I hadn't actually seen her for many years. Sadly, like many of my friends from school, we had simply lost touch as college and working life had taken over. Facebook wasn't invented in those days, so keeping in touch was a lot harder to do.

Despite the many years that had passed, I still felt the devastation of the tragic loss of such an amazing young woman, stolen away so callously.

Many of her school friends reunited in grief at the funeral mass and we all met up in our old sixth form haunt, The Red Lion to raise a glass to Rosie. I don't know if anything since has truly made me feel like an adult, in the way her death did.

Since then I have stood graveside for far too many people that were stolen too soon. Holding the hands of friends who have lost, partners, parents, siblings and sadly the worst loss of all, a child.

Even life's big occasions, weddings, births, first day at school, push us a little bit closer to that realisation that we are indeed the so called, sensible, mature middle-aged people that society depends on. We hold down jobs, raise families, keep the local youth, sports, and scouting clubs going with our endless hours of volunteering, trip planning and car-pooling, all for the good of our own offspring, but also our communities as a whole - 'children are the future' after all!

Sometimes though, it all feels a little bit like an out of body experience, and I actually feel totally disconnected from all of the grown-up things I'm doing, almost like a puppet being operated by someone else.

Being a parent, especially to a child with special needs, makes you grow up fast, but still sometimes it just doesn't feel real. We all face into the typical signs and signals of adulthood, like bills, mortgages, sensible shoes with a low heel, without so much as blinking an eyelid. It all goes by seamlessly and before we know it, we all have, fuel efficient SUVs, a coveted tracker mortgages and are holding out for Black Friday to buy an amply discounted pair of Ecco shoes and a Smart TV - all the staples of a grown-up life. We have to face facts and get real, you can't wear heels on the side-lines of a football pitch, not unless you're a WAG, and let's face it they never have to be pitch side worrying about keeping their good jeans clean.

Occasionally, I take a step back looking at my house or car and think, bloody hell, I own that, or at least I do on paper, even if the monthly payments catapulting from my bank account on payday, rein me in a bit and remind me, that actually I nearly, own it at least!

When I was a child, I would ask my Nana how old she was and be shocked that she was in her sixties. She would tell me every birthday, "I don't feel any different."

I have to admit to being totally perplexed by that comment every year.

This wrinkly little old lady, who always had baking flour on her polyester trousers from Marks and Spencer, she slept with her teeth in a glass and wore a psychedelic floral swim hat, anytime we went to the pool. How could she not 'feel' like she was pushing one hundred years old. But now, of course, I completely get it.

On holiday, in France this year, a little girl wandered passed me with a rubber ring that had a mermaid's tail and I was right back to being 7 again! I so desperately wanted to have that rubber ring. I had to quickly remind myself that a) I am 43 years old and b) There wasn't a hope in hell that a rubber ring, designed for children, was ever going around my waist. Middle age spread is the largest and most visual sign of my adulthood, so getting it passed my arse or boobs would be like trying to pass a rottweiler guarding its master - painful and likely to end in tears and blood - both of them mine. So, Nana, now I absolutely get what you meant.

As the years roll by, speeding up with each passing birthday, our brains take a while to catch up. Maybe our resistance to this and the desire to never truly feel like a grown up is rooted in us not wanting to miss out on the fun. Or to face the terrifying fact, that like a great party you don't ever want to leave, our one great truth, is one day, someone will be shedding tears at our grave side. The fact that, none of us are getting out alive, is the part of adulthood we all fight hard to avoid.

So whilst, I won't be missing any payments on my

tracker mortgage and the school lunches will continue to be packed sensibly every day, ensuring the right mix of dairy, fruit and grains, you won't be stopping me having a sneaky go on the slide in the park, looking out the window checking for Santa on Christmas Eve or licking the bowl when we make cakes.

So, I wonder if I could get that mermaid ring comes in extra-large?

Trying Times

I have an almost five-year age gap between Patrick and Erin. We never planned it that way, but as we all know life has a habit of making its own mind about the plans we make. I thought three or so years would be a good age difference, but lots of things delayed the arrival of our third child.

One rainy August afternoon everyone in Bank of America, Ireland, the company my husband and I worked for, was brought into a conference room, to be told the business was being sold and the future of the Ireland office was in doubt.

Many marriages had formed in MBNA and many a mortgage signed off on the strength of our salaries, so there were a lot of worried sighs in the room. I was sitting directly behind Mick and I wanted to cry, but I stopped myself by focusing on the top of his shirt and wishing I was better at ironing because it looked like screwed up paper.

After a lot of soul searching about whether we should contemplate a third baby if we were both going to be unemployed, we decided that we would stick to plan as I don't think Mick could have handled my tears and tantrums if we didn't. I was lucky and got pregnant quite quickly, but sadly I miscarried at seven weeks.

I convinced myself it would be fine as long as I got pregnant again straight away, but I didn't, and it wasn't fine. The day my period arrived the first time after the miscarriage, I sat at my desk at work, literally unable to move, sobbing inconsolably and needed to take a month off work.

You can run from grief, but it will always catch up to you eventually. Five months later whilst away on holidays I reached the day my period was due and then passed it. I was hopeful, but terrified running to the toilet every three minutes just to check it hadn't appeared. We arrived home on my second 'late day' and I couldn't survive the two-hour trip to Leitrim without knowing if I was pregnant or not. I went to Dundrum shopping centre and bought a test. I peed in a plastic sandwich container to take the test. I was in the loo for ages and with all the rustling and the little shriek of joy I gave when the test was positive, people probably thought I was in there shooting up Class A drugs.

Devastatingly, that pregnancy also ended up with a miscarriage at ten weeks. We had a healthy scan at eight weeks, so that news totally blindsided me and was a total shock as it was a missed miscarriage (no bleeding). I had to have what used to be known as a D&C, now loving re-titled as an ERPC – which means Excavation of Retained Products of Conception. Whichever insensitive soul came up with that heartless title has never made it onto my Christmas Card list!

I was pretty much catatonic for the few days afterwards. I've only ever seen Mick cry twice and this was one of them. It was just one single tear, but it said it all. My doctor said I should stop trying for a while, but I'm no quitter and like a dog with a bone, I just had to carry on.

I started peeing on expensive sticks called ovulation predictor kits (I've always liked to plan ahead) and became obsessive about optimum conception times in my cycle, poor Mick threatened to go on strike one morning when I set my alarm for 5.30am and woke him up for a baby bonk.

But my dedication paid off and I found out I was pregnant for the fifth time at the end of September 2012. It was the morning Mick and I were due to fly out for a short break to Ibiza. As delighted as I was, I was slightly miffed that I had to abstain from holiday cocktails, but I think Mick was glad of a rest after I'd made him by sex slave for the previous three months. I was absolutely bloody terrified of another miscarriage and regularly suffered panic attacks. The fact that I knew stress could be bad for my baby meant that I then, worried more about being worried – the typical vicious cycle of anxiety that many of you will recognise.

I balled my eyes out when I heard the heartbeat at my twelve-week scan. I have always thought, and still do that that is the most beautiful sound in the world. My pregnancy progressed well and despite being a few days late our beautiful Erin arrived in June 2013. Despite being very common (1 in 4 pregnancies), miscarriage is still not talked about by so many women and certainly fewer men.

It's a silent torture that many go through. I can only begin to imagine how truly devastating that a late miscarriage, still birth or infant loss is. I also feel, that not enough attention is given to the loss of those babies conceived through IVF, that do not develop into a pregnancy. I was lucky not to have to use IVF, but I am sure, in the mind and heart of a hopeful, prospective parent, that baby is your baby, your hopes, your dreams, a part of your future and that loss should always be acknowledged.

After each miscarriage, I found the platitudes people would offer, to be completely and utterly head-wrecking. I know people are trying to help but telling someone who has just experienced a pregnancy loss, that "it wasn't the baby for you" is worthy of a headbutt, in my personal opinion. No matter how short a time they were with us, they were and always will be our babies.

As time passed, I have accepted that if the miscarriages hadn't happened then we wouldn't have our little Erin, and that is a world I can never imagine, but I still do think of the two babies we lost. Everything I have of them, including scan pictures are buried under a tree in our back garden, which interestingly gets the most visits from my Dad.

To remember them we bought a star and named it Seren Hayden (Seren means star in my native Welsh). I often say hello when I am outside in the evenings. It's true that what doesn't kill us makes us stronger and that life goes on, but my personal advice when looking for the right words to say to someone in this situation is not to use the 'usual but useless' words of wisdom. But simply let the person know that you care about their loss and that their baby matters. That is what helped me.

I would like to dedicate this piece to my friends Debbie and Tony Murphy who lost their baby son Jake in 2011. Thank you for giving me and so many people a space to grieve and remember our lost babies.

If you have been impacted by infant or pregnancy loss, then you can receive support from people with lived experience at www.féileacáin.ie

Women's Intuition

Patrick said his first word at 13 months old. He was at his Granny's house in Dublin looking at a picture of our dog and shouted out "gog". He didn't say much more for many months after that. He'd had a runny nose since the day he was born and the mucous river that continued to flow, had caused him to get glue ear. He had grommets inserted when he was 21 months old, within four days he had twelve new words. Including rugby and football – his Daddy was so proud! My favourite toddler word of Patrick's was "lella" it took us a while to figure out that it meant – banana (because they are yellow).

Patrick's first smile had appeared at seven weeks old and continued to grow. His smile lit up a room, always brightening my day. Although ironically my favourite picture of him is with a super serious head on him, looking like he might punch someone – sadly that was to become a look we would see a lot.

During his first two years on this earth, Patrick showed none of the more well-known signs of Autism. But by the time he was two and a half I just knew something was different. I had no idea what exactly.

I just knew!

Patrick was always a very 'busy' child, he definitely puts the boy in boisterous and as an only child myself I thought initially this was just part of life with a boy child. His behaviour always made me question my abilities as a parent. Saoirse has been a textbook child and I thought I had good control on her development and behaviour, but to me Patrick was a puzzle that often had me tearing my hair out.

As you've read earlier, he destroyed, plants, car windscreens and oven doors as a toddler. He was often destructive, loud and wild and had would have some fierce temper tantrums. He would never sit for very long, particularly at the dinner table, and we regularly had to chase after him to get to him into his seat or lift him down off the table.

I became increasingly worried that he had ADHD. My husband didn't see any major issue, he is the second boy of five, who were then followed by three girls. Compared to my sedate upbringing as an only child, Mick's family seemed semi feral. Stories of throwing his youngest brother Shay out of a second- floor bedroom window into the heavy snow of the early-eighties and full on fights with his older brother Pat using pitch forks and horse whips, did scare me somewhat. It sounded a bit like a Quentin Tarantino Movie1

When I struggled with Patrick's behaviour my mother-in-law would regularly tell me "he'll grow out of it, he's just a boy!" When Patrick was being challenging, other Mum's would look at me with mild pity, glad it wasn't their turn to deal with a toddler tantrum. But something was different than a typical tantrum,

I just knew!

In January 2013 we gave Saoirse and Patrick a

beautiful book called "There's a House in Mummy's Tummy" at the back of it was taped a scan picture of their baby sister. I was 20 weeks pregnant. From the very next day, I began to notice a marked change in Patrick's behaviour, and he became a lot more challenging. So much so I went to discuss it with my GP who said we should monitor the situation but, he was probably just unsettled at the thought of a new baby.

Erin arrived in June 2013.

Both Patrick and Saoirse were thrilled, and Patrick got so excited he almost sat on his new baby sister at the hospital. Things progressed reasonably well for the first few months but when Patrick started school that September, we could see he was really struggling. He made it through to the mid-term break relatively unscathed, but when he went back in November all hell broke loose. He would cope reasonably well at school but going to the toilet 15-20 times a day to avoid sitting in his seat.

At home in the evenings his distress would erupt into hysterical tantrums, that would often last for upwards of three hours. He would punch, kick, bite, throw things and just generally be impossible to deal with. Every night felt like audition for 'Super Nanny' – the certificate 18 version.

Dealing with this and a teething five-month old was something of a challenge. I don't think Saoirse got a bedtime story for that whole month. Not a huge issue I know, but it makes me sad to think that she had to learn at the tender age of seven, that her needs would often not be Mum and Dad's top priority.

After Patrick's behaviour escalated nightly for six long weeks, we finally decided to go to our GP. She referred us to CAMHS (Child and Adolescent Mental Health Services for those of you lucky enough to not have heard of it – I genuinely hope you never have to), and so began our tumultuous relationship with 'the system.' But no matter how much they would fob us off,

I just knew!

The A Word

We felt hopeful of a resolution to the enigma that was Patrick, when we entered 'the system' in 2013. But that hope quickly waned and was replaced by frustration and desperation.

After multiple appointments where Psychologists changed their minds every five minutes and reports didn't match up and so-called professionals couldn't find our notes and blah blah *blag*, we were told in May 2015 that Patrick couldn't have ADHD.

This was a decision we queried because, although the questionnaire we as parents filled in showed he definitely did with 99% probability, the questionnaire from his schoolteacher showed he didn't. I did point out that I felt the school report may not be accurate as the teacher the previous year definitely saw issues and the teacher filling in the form, apparently did not like 'labels'. But it was decided that, as Patrick had sat calmly for the full three minutes, he was in with the CAMHS Psychiatrist assessing him, he apparently couldn't possibly have ADHD!

In the weeks afterwards when I mulled and festered over the experience, I wondered could he have Autism as he wasn't great at explaining what he was feeling, didn't mix well with children his own age and really didn't cope well with change. I dismissed the idea, thinking the Psychiatrist and Psychologists we had seen, would have picked up on it if he did.

Patrick's behaviour and abilities at school and home

continued to be a challenge and I regularly contacted the Assessment of Needs Officer, about supports and a possible re-assessment, but was told there was no one 'in post' to re-assess Patrick. Leitrim was without a CAMHS professional for over two years!

I consider Leitrim to be the constipated county of Ireland - because nobody gives a shit. I called multiple times to follow up on the Play and Speech and Language Therapy support we had been promised, but it came to nothing. On one particular day when Patrick had thrown a kitchen stool at me, I was weary and upset and a smart-arsed secretary in CAMHS told be abruptly, maybe I needed to do a parenting course. Two words sprang to mind and one of them was off, I'll let you fill in the blank!

For those of you familiar with 'the system' being sent on a parenting course is the HSE answer to the questions they don't know to answer, and the parenting course will apparently fix ever challenge your child has ever had. Sound far-fetched? It is!

As it happens, I have done four parenting courses, completed an OT therapy course for brain training to assist emotional regulation, gone back to college on weekends and completed a level 7 certificate in Special Educational Needs for SNAs. None of it has made a blind bit of difference for more than a week.

On the guidance of professionals, we have brought Patrick to a dietician, to reflexology, to cranial sacral massage, to SLT, and Occupational Therapy.

We have bought sensory toys, essential oils, yoga CDs, mindfulness books, a punch bag, trampolines big and small – we have tried it all and almost bankrupted ourselves in the process. All with little to no effect. I'm beginning to wonder if they have shares in these solutions?

In July 2016 someone suggested Patrick be checked for Dyslexia, this was a new avenue we hadn't considered. 4 weeks and €500 later, we met with the Educational Psychologist who told us that Patrick had both Dyslexia and Dyscalculia, much like ordering food a Mexican restaurant the words are hard to pronounce and impossible to spell for the person with the learning difficulty.

The Educational Psychologist told us Patrick's dyslexia meant was in the bottom 1-2% of the population and gave us a list of possible supports that would see him right through to his 99th birthday! For anyone who has ever seen one of these reports, finding the right place to start supporting your child is like finding that infamous needle in a haystack.

But try we did, again a small fortune spent on the right books the right pencils etc. As chairwoman of the school parents' association I organised a parents training session and allocated funds for special high/low readers so the dyslexic children in the school could enjoy the library too. I'm a big believer in inclusivity and based on current statistics, it was likely that 20-40 children in the 200-pupil school Patrick attended at the time, actually had dyslexia or some kind of reading delay.

Patrick's report meant he was entitled to more significant support from the resource teacher, a laptop for school and an Irish exemption (Mick was gutted about this bit). We hoped that this support would help Patrick academically, but more importantly help to alleviate the frustration dyslexic people often feel and reduce the aggression at home. It didn't! His resource teacher also alerted us to her concerns about what she called 'developmental delays'. We (we as in my wonderful husband, Mick, as I had long lost patience with doing Patrick's homework after he stabbed me in the leg with a pencil) diligently worked through Dolch lists and 'Toe by Toe' every night. Patrick made excellent progress and even began to write in a reasonably straight line. We were super proud of him and more importantly, he was proud of himself. But we were still seeing a lot of aggression and an increasing amount of anxiety.

On the day of his Communion, Patrick refused to get out of the car and when he did, he attached himself, limpet like to Mick's leg. We don't have any pictures of Patrick smiling at the church. I also had my first truly heart-breaking moment that day, when I observed the other 7 boys in Patrick's class huddle together for a selfie as Patrick sat sadly at the end of the aisle as he wasn't invited to be in it. It took every ounce of strength I had not to show my upset and anger. I held back the tears, but my eyes were shooting out daggers!

That summer, as we were filling in yet another round of

forms for a further assessment, this time privately as there was still no-one 'in post' in CAMHS (someone send a Psychiatrist or some Senacot please!) Patrick's class teacher stuck a post-it-note on the form saying she had concerns he was going to slip through the cracks in the system.

We decided that day it was time to move schools. The school he was in is a decent school with some fantastic teachers, but it was just too big to suit Patrick's particular needs. We applied for Patrick to go to a small, 35 pupil school locally. This was without doubt the best move we ever made for our son. It is not a special needs school, but it is most definitely a special school. Although Patrick was full of anxiety and didn't want to go, he was super brave and went anyway and settled really well.

The Principal's condition of him going to the school, was that he would start in second class, repeating the year he had just completed. Given Patrick's challenges we felt this was a great idea and would give him the chance to settle before the big leap to third class.

That summer we went privately for a basic assessment of Patrick's behaviour found him to have a Sensory Processing Disorder and also definite signs of ADHD – so more forms to fill in! The Psychologist also broached the subject of an Autism Assessment, Mick and I decided we would let him settle into his new school, before going through yet another assessment. Patrick liked his new school and made friends quickly, although he got on best with the little ones in Junior Infants. He had always got on better with the younger ones. When he was in Montessori, in the afternoons he like to go into the baby room and sing to the babies and at family parties he always hangs out with his younger cousins – they all adore him. I didn't know this at the time, but not being comfortable or competent in your own age group and gravitating towards much younger people, is an Autistic trait. Things were good at school, until the November Nightmare reared its ugly head again. This time, it was so much worse because Patrick was so much bigger and stronger, plus he'd learned some every interesting swear words, which he liked to lob at us along with other items from his bedroom like money boxes, photo frames, books – anything that came to hand.

Patrick continued to punch, kick, spit, bite and roar but he also decided it would be fun to spice things up a bit with weapons – books, curtain poles, tennis racquets. Anything left lying around or within his reach could be cultivated into a weapon of mass destruction. Back to the GP and back to CAMHS we went, fortunately they had got their act together and had employed a fantastic new Psychiatrist. She saw our stress and need straight away. This time Patrick's ADHD questionnaires from school and home matched up with 99% and 93% probability of ADHD. So, he received an official diagnosis.

Like so many parents in our situation, this actually came as a huge relief. It meant Patrick needed help and support that he would now be eligible for, it meant we weren't going mad and most importantly for me, it meant I wasn't a bad mother. Which for so many years I had thought I must be.

The Psychiatrist felt he was showing a lot of Autistic traits and should be assessed, and although we had been in 'the system' for 4 years by then, it had never entered anyone's head to put Patrick on a waiting list for one.

Due to distinct lack of laxatives or mental health professionals being sent to Leitrim there was still nothing happening and the waiting list of up to 2 years. We decided we had to go privately and as Mick had just got his annual bonus, luckily, we didn't have to make another withdrawal from the bank of Mum and Dad to foot the hefty bill. We went back to Dublin for the assessment, to the Treehouse Practice in Sandyford for the assessment which was very comprehensive and required three trips and a forest worth of forms to be completed – but if you're going to do something, do it right. Especially something as potentially life changing as this.

And so, one rainy Thursday night in March 2018, I took the phone call to be told, yes Patrick did in fact meet the criteria for Autism.

We were not relieved, but nor were we shocked. For me in particular I had known for many years something was different. I had been running an Autism youth club for several years and was in the middle of my SNA training course, so by that stage, with reasonable knowledge and experience of Autism, I had a fair idea that he would meet the criteria.

Mick on the other hand was pretty surprised, he had told himself that Patrick wasn't Autistic and much like every year when he tells himself in February, Ireland will win the six nations – he couldn't possibly be wrong. I'm not slagging Mick in a bad way, but I think the diagnosis was probably like receiving the news of a multiple birth.

What I love about Mick though is that he is the least judgmental person I have ever met. I knew the diagnosis would never be any kind of issue to him. It was a shock to many of our friends and family, as Patrick like so many other kids with High Functioning Autism, seems perfectly fine in many situations and only as he has gotten older are people beginning to see his differences. So many parents of children with similar issues to Patrick tell me they have faced the same situation with people's perception. The concerns of thousands of parents are being regularly ignored, meaning diagnoses are being missed every day, by the professionals we trust to get these things right. A child Psychologist told me recently, that new research suggests, that in 85% of cases where the mother of a child had a 'gut feeling' something was different or wrong – she is right. That lived experience, intuition or the fact that sometimes' mother knows best' simply cannot be ignored any longer, because it is the safety and well-being of our children that is at stake.

Right Here, Right Now

As this decade comes to an end, I cannot begin to describe how awful it has been in so many ways, not just for us but for every one of my close friends. So much of what my friends have experienced have been sadly and devastatingly unavoidable. Two of my close friends have lost their partners to cancer, one friend suffering it herself more than once, job losses, and a variety of other weird, but never wonderful events, that have made these 21st century teen years, pretty unbearable.

Sadly though, our situation is a little different. I firmly believe that a lot of what we have been through could have been reduced greatly, if Patrick had gotten the care and support that he needed back in 2013 when we first flagged his behaviour difficulties to 'the system'.

I can see now, with that wonderful little tool of hindsight, that Patrick was showing signs of Autism from a much earlier age than I realised. The earlier the intervention an Autistic person receives, the better their outcomes. It is like most other conditions, physical or intellectual, the earlier you know and take action, the better.

To protect his privacy, I have made a conscious decision not to go into graphic detail about Patrick's meltdowns. I will discuss the challenges faced by many Autistic people in this regard, in a later chapter, because I do feel raising awareness of this ultimate taboo, is vital in developing people's understanding of how these challenges can be reduced and dealt with. This, in my humble opinion is how we will achieve true inclusion.

I am an Autism Advocate, but I cannot accept that means agreeing that Autism is not a disability. It is at times severely disabling for my son and many other Autistic people. Autism is not a disease that people suffer from, but at times people suffer as a result of the symptoms or presentations of Autism. What each of my children, and we as parents have experienced for the last 7 years, is devastating and exhausting for anyone to deal with and for the last 2 years it has been pretty much constant.

I recently attended a Beyond Limits Summit in Dublin, with a presentation, from a man named Jack Kavanagh, who is a wheelchair user and disabilities advocate stated, that the biggest disabler, is the environment disabled people are in. We have found this is most certainly true. The lack of supports that are offered to people with disabilities and their families is neglectful of their basic human rights, to a dangerous level.

The most vulnerable people in our society, who need significant extra support to fulfil the daily functions, that so many of us take for granted, are given very limited tools to support them. Their families, in addition to providing extra daily care, have to continuously pull on their body armour and find the energy from their already depleted resources, to go into a battle for services. We have to beg, please, demand and basically humiliate ourselves in a variety of ways to try and make our voices heard.

Dealing always, with the guilt of knowing that if you shout loudest, you are drowning out the voice of an equally needy person. This year, I gave up my job to fight this battle. I have had to involve the national media, local politicians, government ministers and threaten legal action.

3 times this year, I have presented at HSE buildings with a sleeping bag, refusing to leave until we get listened to and secured services that we are desperate for. Always packing my fanciest 'sleepover' Pyjamas in case my protest ends up in the newspaper. Often the agreed services and supports we are given, get cancelled or reduced soon after.

We are very fortunate that we have the financial means for me to take a year off work, and that with my business background I have the skillset I need to take on the hardened and brainwashed guardians of 'the system'. Many people are not that lucky, what happens to their needs?

The impact of this struggle, on my own physical and mental health, has come close to catastrophic. I totally broke down in Aldi recently, when some neighbours asked how things were going for Patrick bursting into floods of tears. My tear and snot stained face in the middle of the supermarket is not a look I generally go for whilst shopping, preferring a lightly made up face, with smart, fashionable eye wear to complete my look.

I am deeply saddened and angry that our beautiful little boy did not get the support he needed for six long years. Six years where he has been screaming in pain, for help through his behaviour. Six years where we have told 'the system' over and over again that we desperately need their support, our pleas, backed up by teaching staff and therapists.

Early intervention, would, in my opinion have made a significant difference to our circumstances. My 6-year-old daughter, has never known anything but this difficult life, and now experiences the effects of trauma. My, teenage daughter has been forced to deal with situations, no adult should even have to. All three of our beautiful children, are completely blameless in the situation we find ourselves in and all three are at risk, a risk that could be mitigated.

There have been days when I feel I have completely lost my dignity as I've acted banshee like to try and get anyone to pay any kind of attention to our needs and give us some kind of help.

My daughter, Saoirse recently read 'The Hunger Games'. I think the book may actually be based on the Irish Health Service. Children and young people are being left to fight for their lives. The resources are unfairly distributed, so some have a much better chance of survival that others. The people involved have to fight every step of the way to make any progress and if you live in District 12 (Rural Ireland) you're deemed as insignificant, disposable even. Left to feel that you are pretty much screwed from the start.

The odds, are never in our favour. Just like Katniss Everdeen, I will fight to the death for my people!

It's just a shame that I have to!

WTF Are You Talking About?

I used to work for large American Corporate Bank, in England. It was full of very talented, capable people but also quite a few who simply though they were.

To make the dull meetings a little more entertaining and maintain our waning attention, my more mischievous friends and I used to engage in a game of 'bullshit bingo', marking our page every time someone used one of the current 'buzz phrases'. You know the type I mean, those phrases that some numpties think sound good but don't actually mean anything of any value.

In the new abbreviated world, that we now seem to live in, I have needed to adapt my ears to a new kind of language, again much of it meaningless to my forty-something brain.

Deciphering my children's text messages or conversations to try and pick up on what they may mean. Fortunately, none of my children have never watched TOWIE (The Only Way is Essex), so we've avoided that particular destruction of the English language and are never "well jel" and the only "totes" we use, come with handles. I'm afraid though I have succumbed to the use of many acronyms, often having to ask my tween daughter to translate.

My absolute favourite of all, and invented by and for middle aged women has to be FFS. This darling little phrase is my saviour of sanity on many occasions, and uttering it under my breath or in a speech bubble in my head has helped me to maintain composure when dealing with many a total PITA (Pain in the Arse).

As a parent to a child with special needs, the use of Acronyms is mind boggling, often to the point of making me d.i.z.z.y. I have become quite well versed in this new language in recent years and feel I could put it on my CV along with intermediate German and basic French. Although, I'm not sure if knowing how to order a large glass of white wine whilst on a city break in Paris, is maybe a little too basic for what employers are looking for!

I'm afraid much like a parent of a new-born, dreamily starting every conversation with a new tale of their precious and shiny new offspring, I am a total Autism bore and somehow almost every conversation I have, meanders towards it at some point. I see my friend's eyes glaze over as a vague look of 'oh no, not again' flashes across their faces. Although if Patrick's behaviour has been particularly challenging, they may find my stories a bit more interesting. as their woes of "well Amelia just won't eat peas anymore" never measure up to the wild world of my trainee ninja!

Most of my good friends, know the SEN (special education needs), acronyms by now, as they are so used to me using them, but I have to remember that to most people it is complete mumbo jumbo that I am speaking, as fortunately for them, they don't live in the crazy world I inhabit. But as 1 in 65 school age children in Ireland are now diagnosed with Autism, never mind any other syndromes or conditions that often go along with it, it's a language we all will, no doubt become familiar with. So, here are a few of the basics to get you started:

CAMHS - Child and Adolescent Mental Health Services

ASD - Autism Spectrum Disorder

ADHD - Attention Deficit Hyperactivity Disorder

OT/PT/SALT - Occupational Therapist/Physical Therapist/Speech And Language Therapist

SENO - Special Educational Needs Officer

SNA - Special Needs Assistant (at school or preschool)

IEP - Individualised Education Programme/Plan

STIM - Self Stimulatory Behaviour (e.g. rocking, pacing, tapping, screeching)

DSM 5 - Diagnostic Statistics Manual Version 5 (the bible of diagnosing any SEN)

But as with any language, there is always a particular dialect depending on what part of the special needs community you are from. I sat down with Patrick's Clinical Psychologist a few weeks ago, to be told that Patrick presented with a particular kind of Autism profile. OH, that was new, I thought Tinder was where you would find profiles, and at 11 he's a bit young for that carry on!

But, the golden fact of Autism is that, everyone's Autism is different to them, it is unique and presents in different ways. Patrick, for example, has rarely struggled verbally, that is one of the reasons why, his diagnosis was so delayed. Patrick has a PDA and ODD profile, Pathological Demand Avoidance and Oppositional Defiance Disorder. Without blinding you with science, what that basically means is that Patrick gets hugely anxious, and I mean absolutely terrified, by so many of the basic things we do every day. Things that most of us take for granted, he will avoid doing whatever it is, by whatever means necessary.

Going to school being one of the biggest challenges he faces. Being as fearful about going to school as I would be about wrestling a crocodile - literally. This is very hard to understand, as he loves his school, his friends, his teachers and his beloved SNA, the wonderful Roisin, who is providing 121 support for most of the day. But still, like so many Autistic children, it causes him an insane amount of anxiety.

Secondly, Patrick will often do the exact opposite of anything you want him to do. To the point of seeking out extremely annoying, harmful and unpleasant behaviours to get a reaction, particularly from me, because I am his 'safe space'. This is NOT because he is bad or naughty, but his brain actually, needs, the release the negative reaction brings, simply to be able to function. Autism is very complicated!

Sadly, as part of his particular profile, Patrick struggles with the worst acronym of all. SEND VCB - Special Educational Needs and Disabilities related, Violent/Challenging Behaviours. That's a huge title, and a huge part of our lives. This is the part of life with special needs, some, but not all, people experience, that you will never see on a poster of a cute child with some syndrome or other.

This is the part of special needs that is understandably, kept a secret by so many. Personally, it is something I am open about, in fact I try to raise awareness about it. Because this is not Patrick's fault, this does not make Patrick a bad person and most importantly, this is something that can be supported and massively reduced with the right therapy and the right adjustments in place in the wider society.

In my experience so far, in the UK and Ireland, and no doubt around the world, it suits governments perfectly well that this part of SEN is not discussed, because then they don't have to fund support for it.

They choose to leave families, like ours, struggling with it, on their own, figuring it out with their TRIBE (not an acronym, but what you call the invaluable group of other SEN parents who are your lifeline).

To be honest, after reading the chapters in this part of the book, I'm sure you'll understand why, the biggest acronym I have used this decade is WTF!

We all know what that one means, and we all need to be asking wannabe politicians, that call to our door, WTF they are doing to support people with disabilities in meaningful ways and WTF are they thinking, making an already difficult life harder, almost to the point of being intolerable and even dangerous. WT actual F?! Just maybe substitute the F for Flip, you don't want to upset their delicate little ears.

Now back to that little bit of French on my CV. One large glass of white wine please!

For anyone impacted by or experiencing SEND VCB there is an excellent, closed (private) Facebook group of the same name, that offers a safe space for families in this situation to talk, exchange ideas etc. It has been my lifeline this year. It is run by a lady with lived experience of SEND VCB, who on her website www.yvonnenewbold.com offers explanations, solutions and support - but never judgement.

Alternative Breathing Apparatus

Mindfulness as a practice, has really taken a hold in the last decade. Although like many positive ideas or practices, once big business gets involved it seems to lose a lot of its intended impact and feels a little contrived.

I tried yoga when I was pregnant with Erin, but I have to admit that it actually had the opposite effect, as I would worry that I might fart when doing downward dog or I'd upset with myself when I couldn't clear my mind and would find myself thinking of baby names or Friday's dinner menu whilst doing yoga Nidra.

The same thing happened, when I went to a mini meditation workshop at an event I attended recently. I really wasn't fussed, but I was bored with walking around the stands. I arrived a bit late, which no doubt messed with the energy in the room, but no one was allowed to glare at me, because a) they were supposed to have their eyes closed and b) negative energy towards a fellow participant totally fucks with your Chakra - I don't know if it does, I made that up, I'm not even sure what a Chakra is.

But just like yoga, I was very easily distracted by other stuff going on. For one, we had to take our shoes off to be grounded with the floor. I had on odd socks, had been travelling in Dublin traffic, therefore had sweaty, probably slightly smelly feet and I hadn't painted my toe-nails in weeks. Therefore, my willingness to reveal my feet to a room full of strangers was a little restricted.

I did it slowly under silent protest, hoping no one would open their eyes long enough to see my nasty toenails, and gave in to the sound of the lady's voice. She was not Irish and I spent most of my time, trying to figure out where her accent was from, technically, I was doing what she was asking and listening to her voice! It would have been ok, and pretty relaxing until she started hitting the gong. It wasn't that it was loud or intrusive, it was just that it reminded me of the opening notes of the title song in Peaky Blinders and nothing about the Shelby Family, in any way lends itself to peace and harmony.

The staple of relaxation, is deep breaths. There is a smorgasbord of ways to calm your breathing, it's like Tapas for the enlightened. Whatever method you select, from your Mindfulness App of choice, it is guaranteed to slow your heart rate and help restore calm. The only problem is, that when life is so hectic and if like me, you are dealing with one emergency and mini trauma after another, the effect of deep breathing loses its impact.

You get to the point that to cope, you have to breath so deep, you'll be breathing out of you of your ass for it to make any difference. At least Ass Breathing is a novel trick for the party you go to.

Never Have I Ever

I remember a lovely trip over to my home in Wales when I was 6 months pregnant on Saoirse. My Mum and I spent a lovely afternoon in Mamas and Papas at the local retail park.

I think the shop assistant that helped us that day made a week's salary in commission just from our one visit. I bought it all, multi-purpose pram/pushchair/car-seat, a Moses basket, cot, baby bath etc. etc. and a wardrobe full of neutral coloured clothes as I didn't yet know the gender of my baby. This is back in the day when gender neutral clothing meant Babygro's lemon and mint.

Like many prospective parents, I spent a second mortgage on stuff that my new baby couldn't live without and an equally large financial investment in stuff that would never come of the box, only to be re-gifted to other clueless first-time parents at a later date.

I look back fondly at how naïve I was about what kind of parent I would never be and I think of the game, Never Have I Ever – this is what I planned to be able to say, before I actually had children:

Never Have I Ever:

- Given my children sweets before the age of seven.

- Let my children watch TV for more than 30 minutes at a time.

- Allowed Dan TDM to babysit.

- Given them a cereal bar for breakfast so I could go back to bed.

- Wiped their nose with a sock.

As real life took hold, I realised this parenting lark is not at all simple, and we all make concessions that start off small and grow much bigger with the arrival of each bundle of joy. My favourite parenting joke has always been:

If your first child eats mud, you take them to hospital.

If your second child does it, you wash their mouth out.

If your third child does it, you wonder if you need to give lunch!

But life, being life, none of us can have any idea what is around the corner of the parenting block. As an Autism parent, you have to go right back to parenting school and re-think it all. Communication style is different, consequences are different, planning days out is different. It's all alien to anything at all you had ever imagined.

Unfortunately, due to very extreme nature of my son's Autism Meltdowns, my 'Never Have I Ever' list has become completely unrecognisable to even the most hardened parenting veterans. The statements I now have to make are no longer something to smile poignantly over. I can no longer say, Never Have I Ever:

- Had to fix a door my son has kicked in.

- Agreed that our family needed support from a social worker.

- Agreed to give my 9-year-old child anti-anxiety and anti-psychotic medication and daily sedatives to control him.

- Worried that my son may end up in prison.

- Been so desperate, I've shamefully, screamed and sworn down the phone to make sure my son gets the basic supports he needs.

Life changes dramatically when you have a child with special needs, sometimes people must think I'm vying for a role in EastEnders when I tell then what is going on in our lives. Often, Patrick is a funny, charming, gentle little boy who is an absolute joy to be around. Everyone that meets him loves him, because he is just so sweet. When living in the world of Autism, you truly have to be prepared for your parenting motto to be 'never say never.'

Labour of Love

Like all women, I love a good labour story.

Whenever women get together for long periods of time, we inevitably swap stories of how bad it got. I was lucky enough to have three quick labours. Obviously, they were all tough and I deserved a medal or at least a bunch of flowers on each of them – I am still waiting on both items from my husband though! My friend, Christine, definitely wins the best 'hard labour' story.

On her second son, she got up at 1am to go to the toilet. She felt a strange sensation, so on her way back to bed, she looked in her full-length mirror, only to see a tiny foot peeping out. After a horrifying ambulance ride to the hospital, she had enough breath left to make sure she was suitably covered so that the whole of A&E didn't see her backside, after being knocked out for an emergency C section she woke up to her perfect little boy.

Labour is not easy; the clue is in the name! But we all know that the end result is worth every ounce of pain.

Once we get home with our bundles of joy the love grows every day. Sometimes as a parent we have bad days, bad moments and we feel we could gladly put our children up for sale on eBay, or at the very least re-locate them to the shed for a little while, but it soon passes.

What I have had to learn as a special needs parent, is that at times, the love for your child can show itself differently to your other children. You are and will always be the biggest advocate for your child. Unfortunately, as 'the system' is so stacked against people whose needs are in any way 'different', then you often to have to use up much of your valuable time and energy being that advocate.

The last 2 years, have definitely been our most challenging time. Last year. At the end of the summer holidays, Patrick put a pillow over my face and tried to suffocate me, whilst I was asleep.

Although he is fully verbal, he could not find any other way to tell me how scared or upset he was about returning to school. This is not just September blues, this is severe, uncontrollable, painful anxiety. After this incident, I found myself emotionally shutting down, making myself feel numb. Without doubt it is a defence mechanism, if I have to think too hard about it then I would crumble and couldn't function for him or anyone else. Sadly, when we do this, there is only one emotional switch and you switch off the positive emotion with the negative.

Just like the endless reviews of the year that appear on our screens and magazine pages during the December, lately, I have sat and contemplated the decade that was coming to an end. I love to trawl through stories and pictures of things I had forgotten.

In all honesty though, both 2018 and 2019 are years that I pretty much want to forget. I had started 2019, feeling positive, hopeful. The Christmas break had been peaceful, even enjoyable.

Patrick's new medication plan was working and things felt, calm. My hopes were smashed by 6pm on New Year's Day. We had friends over for dinner and Patrick became overwhelmed. He had an unmerciful meltdown. Erin finally hit a wall in the way she copes and also had some kind of little breakdown, she was hysterical and hyperventilating, every time she seemed to calm down, she would get upset again. I was in one room dealing with Erin, Mick in another dealing with Patrick. We had to swap every few minutes as they were both screaming for me. I don't know why. Mick is a lot calmer than I am. But whenever Patrick gets really distressed, he only wants for me.

As for Erin, she has always struggled with separation anxiety from me and needed my attention too, and why not every distressed five-year-old just wants their Mummy. This was not an isolated day. The challenges continued pretty much every day of 2019. Autism doesn't know the date, on my birthday, Patrick tipped a full bin of rubbish over my head then hit me with the bin. Not quite the gift I was hoping for, I'd asked for new boots!

My own mental health and ability to cope with these daily challenges often ebbs and flows and I do the best I can. Having peri-menopausal hormones really doesn't help my 'demons', and there are days when I think Mick probably feels he may need to call a priest to do an exorcism.

Earlier this year, after the kids had gone to bed, I totally broke down and told Mick I really didn't know just how much longer I could carry on doing this. Our family has been in crisis for two years now, with 5 years before that being very emotionally draining too. In reality, very few people truly understand what we are dealing with. If you haven't lived it, you just can't know. Through my tears, I told Mick truthfully that, I felt terrified, that I might not love Patrick enough to get us through. I didn't know how much deeper I could dig, to get up every day and face our situation.

This was without a doubt one of my lowest points as a parent. To question the love you have for your child is devastating. I went to bed that night exhausted on every possible level, not knowing if I could even face getting out of bed the next morning.

I did get out of bed the morning after I hit rock bottom, and I have continued to do so. I went to see my GP about it this year and I will forever be grateful to her for not pulling a faux sympathetic face or giving me a hug, instead sitting and listening, talking to me like an adult.

She is a parent herself and asked me, "Is it harder to love Patrick than your girls?" The question took the wind right out of me! Not because I was horrified, but because with that question, she totally validated my feelings. She heard my voice, and I realised I wasn't singing solo!

As a parent, you are supposed to love you child unconditionally, and when you sometimes find that love harder to feel, it comes with a guilt that you continuously carry around like a crushing weight on your chest. The shame of that feeling is crippling. My

GP told me she understood, that this was a natural feeling. Making me realise that I wasn't a monster.

As kind as people are trying to be, when they tell you, "you do an amazing job" or query how they could do it, offering my least favourite platitude "God only give Special Needs kids to special people", these words often make you feel worse. Because inside your head, you don't feel special.

The pressure of being expected to act like a saint, when really that is the last thing in the world you feel like. Sometimes, I don't even want to be anywhere near my children. I want to run away and hide! For once, social media wisdom actually saved me from this particular guilt black hole, telling me that, 'having children is the only time you can experience heaven and hell at the same time.' That phrase nails it for me.

I've come to accept, no one's parenting is anywhere resembling perfect. Does perfect parenting even exist? Much like 'normal', it is a concept that is constantly changing the goal posts. Being a parent is the hardest thing any of us will ever do and being a special needs parent brings new dimensions you never thought possible.

A lot of experts will tell you that you grieve the child you expected to have. I don't know if that is what I am going through but I definitely know it hurts a lot. Some days it makes me feel physically sick and exhausted beyond anything I have ever experienced. I am worn out and worn down. Every day, I aim for good enough, not picture perfect.

I have realised that some days, just getting up out of bed to face your challenges IS enough, and on some days, staying there is the right thing, just as long as you don't stay there too long, and if you do, well then it may be time to consider getting professional support for yourself.

I've done a lot of soul searching over recent weeks, whilst attending much needed therapy, talking it over with the Psychologist and with Heidi the dog as we have walked. I have found a deeper understanding of what I am feeling. I know that I absolutely do love Patrick enough to get us through this. I do love him as much as my girls. However, I have to accept; sometimes that love is in many ways different. That love has changed as the years and challenges have gone by. It is not what I ever expected to feel in my daydreams. That IS ok, because different, is not less. Love does not have to have a particular look or feel to make it right, there really is no rule book.

Love can be strapping your child into a safe car-seat, that you gave up something you enjoyed, to be able to afford.

It can be singing the same song from the Trolls movie over and over for a year, even though it actually now hurts your ears.

It is spending endless hours, day and night, researching, learning, implementing the latest solutions to your child's pain, and it can be calling everybody you can think of; politicians, government ministers, radio presenters, doctors, therapists, giving over every second of your free time, to make sure your child gets the support they so desperately need.

In all truth, many times this year, my love for Patrick has sapped every piece of energy that I have. I often haven't felt the joy I am 'supposed' to, when I'm around him anymore, because if he isn't angry, aggressive or distressed, then I am tense waiting for when he will be. I hate that this part of his Autism, has robbed me of that joy, turned him into someone I often don't recognise.

I and our family, do our very best every day to make things right for Patrick and his sisters, who are also the blameless victims of this situation, making life easier where possible. I know that in doing this, we will find a way to get Patrick's joy back, even if it isn't all the time.

Yesterday, I collected Patrick from my parents' house. He came charging towards me as he always does, shouting my name, so excited to see me. For the first time in a long time, I really enjoyed this moment, feeling real emotion from his embrace, even though he nearly knocked me to the ground! I hope, we are starting to heal.

I will always find a way to get out of bed for each of my children, even if it is not until tea-time some days. Love does conquer all, but it isn't always easy, it isn't like the fairy tales we read. It is giving yourself completely, finding more, even when you thought there was nothing left. Labour doesn't end when our children are born, we owe it them to continue to always push hard, to make sure they survive and thrive in this world.

Thank you for taking the time to read this part of the book. I wish it were fiction, but to us and so many people it is fact. But each and every one of us has the opportunity and the potential to re-write the book and to bring about positive change.

The next part of the book is a lot more light-hearted I promise! Just don't be afraid of the Sock Monster!

Part Three

The Celeriac Crisis

Thε Cεlεriac Crisis

A few weeks ago, I didn't even know what celeriac was, but recently it caused me a crisis! The Celeriac Crisis, it sounds like the title of a Ross O'Carroll Kelly book. Those of you that don't live in Ireland won't get that reference, so for you, it would be the clever title of a book about the first world problems of a Millennial. Both would be on the bestsellers list within a week!

Unbelievably, it was in fact celeriac that recently pushed me over the edge, teetering on the brink of being 'unhinged' completely. It was my son's 11th birthday and it had started at 4.30am, when he came into the bedroom to demand we all get up and open his presents. We cajoled him into our bed and told him, he had a few hours to wait yet.

I'll set the scene; imagine you are going on a 5-hour journey to the ultimate, exciting holiday destination for kids. Imagine, at the start of the journey, you gave your children, 3 energy drinks, a pack of fizzy jellies and a gram of speed, each! Yes, I know, as sensible, caring, educated parents that is of course, unimaginable, but humour me! Use that image to gage the level of energy related torture you would then endure on that 5-hour journey. Well now you have an idea of what it is like trying to keep a child with Autism and ADHD contained in bed, when they are excited about an impending event. The good old Irish phrase 'madder than a bag of cats' springs to mind! That hopefully gives you an indication of how my day started, before I even got out of bed.

It didn't get any better after that. Patrick being up so early was in an awful mood, and was extremely demanding and swearing like a sailor with Tourette's, at anything and everyone from his sisters to his new Lego. He isn't a naughty or mean child, but this belligerent and often offensive behaviour is a part of the make-up of many Autistic people, that, no sensory friendly hour at the supermarket is ever going to cure. To be honest, most of the issues Autistic people face aren't much helped by that music free hour at the supermarket either! But the effort is appreciated.

The saga continued when, whilst trying to stop Patrick from denting himself or my car from punching it, the door of the car boot dropped on my head, nearly knocking me out. The hysteria that then ensued with my 3 children as I cried in agony and tried in vain to gain composure, caused us to be late for school. As the day went on, I managed to drop my new €300 phone down the toilet, stained my favourite new pink hoody, with lily pollen! Then to top it all, I weighed celeriac on my newly purchased kitchen scales and realised, what I had eaten for dinner the previous night was more than 20g of carbs, in fact it was double what I had guesstimated, as I didn't have scales to weigh it yesterday.

So bloody what? Why the hell does that matter? I hear you ask.

Well, I follow the Keto Diet, eating just 20g of carbs per day. It is a law that cannot be broken, it is blasphemy!

Punishable by literally gaining 10lbs on weigh day. Going over this figure takes you out of ketosis and ruins all of your dieting hard work.

To give you an example of how serious this is, I nearly had a panic attack 2 weeks ago in the smoothie bar when I realised, I had been given (and drank) the wrong smoothie, which had a whole banana in it. I managed to avert that crisis by stomping up the road at speed, whilst writing a strongly worded complaint in my head. A complaint I never actually wrote because, a) I love the smoothie bar, it's the best place in Carrick, and b) I realised I was being a total diva over a fecking banana! To try and avert the celeriac crisis, I quickly logged onto the UK Keto Community Facebook page – my online Keto Bible, I am also on the Irish version, which is much more fun as it has less fundamentalists. I needed to seek advice from the Keto congregation. The debate raged on for hours and may still be going 5 weeks later. It could not be agreed, just how many carbs were in fact, in the offending root vegetable. Apparently, it all hinges on whether I bought it in Sainsburys or not, I didn't have the heart to tell them we don't even have Sainsburys in Ireland!!

That day, I realised that so far, I have had a Keto crisis with Avocados, debating with myself on every visit to Aldi, if their Avocados are in fact small or medium, and could I get away with having 2 instead of 1 for breakfast?

Bananas, the afore mentioned smoothie debacle.

And Celeriac, of which no one can give me a definitive

answer as it all hinges on where I shop. As I seem to be working my way through an alphabet of crimes against Keto, I might just say sod it all tomorrow and have a donut, if you're going to do it, do it in style. But, back to the crisis. How many carbs are in a celeriac? This question truly is the epitome of a first world problem. But on that particular day, that smelly, celery root was the straw that broke the camel's back in a day of extreme mayhem.

We all have them, I am sure you could list them off from your day, whether it's a flat battery, a sadistic sat nav or an unintentionally rude comment, from a person whose communication style is simply different from what you are used to.

So often, it's the little things in life that send us hurtling to 'the edge' threatening not to hit the brakes. At those moments, we all just have to take a deep breath, step out of the room for a moment and just try to find the funny side. I promise you it's there if you look hard enough.

P.S If anyone does know the carb content of celeriac that wasn't bought in Sainsbury, please PM me at my Facebook page Bedtime Stories for Mothers and Others

Mental Load

Recently, I dropped my daughter Saoirse at school. Before we left the house, she had been untangling a display of clay planets of our solar system. I'd taken an interest and helped her untangle it, as I vaguely remembered her telling me she had been working on it.

As she got out of the car at the school gate, I said to her "good luck with your planets presentation today." She looked at me a little bit disappointed and answered, "Mum, that was last week, I did tell you."

It may be dramatic to say I was crushed, but I was. It was one of those moments where you feel like the worst Mum in the world, because my mind obviously hadn't been present when my body was and I worry that happens too often these days. I was talking to my good friend about this kind of thing recently. She is a marketeer and knows all of the cool, trendy terms of the moment to sum up my lack of presence.

Apparently, this is now referred to as 'Mental Load'.

It is one of those genius phrases that sums it up perfectly. It is generally the Mum's/Women of the family as opposed to the Dad's/Men that experience Mental Load. I certainly don't mean to sound sexist, but more women tend to be the parent that tunes into the things that contribute to mental load, I think men are generally just oblivious to it. If I were to say to Mick, do you know what day, time and location Taylor's party is on at, he would more than likely say "Who's Taylor?"

rather than given me any information I actually needed. Mental load is usually comprised of the minute, yet key, details of situations and appointments of all varieties, dental, optical, developmental of any kind. Including, but in no way limited to:

• The finer detail such as location, time, allergies, special clothing requirements of every party your child is ever invited to, (and the grudges held for the ones they weren't).

• Knowing what is the 'gift de jour' to buy for yet another birthday celebration, that will appeal to both the child and their parent, neither flashy nor stingy, environmentally sustainable, non-gender specific and most importantly not a re-gift, IF, the original giver of the gift is, actually going to be at the party.

• Who you can car share with to and from the play/art/sport/animal centre that is, for some obscure reason, 40 miles away? Googling the closest Penneys/Primark to see if you can fit a quick trip whilst waiting for the party to be over. This is in fact why going to a children's party can be so expensive.

• Knowing the quickest route, to get from dance class -to- youth club -to- scouts every Tuesday evening, taking into account traffic diversions and train time tables, if passing a level crossing. I have to admit to sometimes realising I'm going in totally the wrong direction and having to keep my panic under control as I say through gritted teeth "it's fine love, we'll make it, teacher doesn't mind if you're a bit late."

- Advance planning of events, confirmations, communions, day trips and breaks away, right down to the size of bag you will need and what is the price difference between sun cream bought in Aldi or bought at the airport.

- Researching the cost, location and effectiveness of shampoo bars to reduce purchases of single-use plastic, making sure we are making a meaningful contribution to the efforts to reduce harmful waste in our seas. I really do have to make some effort in this whole climate change business as, I genuinely am concerned, and simply liking/sharing posts by Greta Thunberg isn't really enough.

- Remembering what kit – PE, swimming, sewing, baking needs to be packed in the school bag for tomorrow (hoping that the usual day hasn't been changed due to bad weather).

- Ensuring the appropriate forms for the school trip/photographs/music lessons/book club is signed and dated and the correct money is sent in, so the school secretary doesn't have to find change of a fifty euro note.

- Making sure that you also have coin change for credit union saving day, raffle tickets, swim lockers etc. This is no mean feat nowadays as we are moving towards a cashless society and Dad's pockets are no longer sagging from the weight of coins of every denomination.

For me personally, it also involves, remembering the

name and birthday of everyone I have ever met. It's control thing, every other element of my life can be going to the wall and one of my children may not have gotten lunch in their school bag that day. But, as long as some random in-law, who I'm not particularly keen on anyway, got their birthday card on time, then, all is fine in my world. I AM IN CONTROL!

Last year I experienced another epic parenting fail, when I forgot to put together the calendars of lovely photographs of my little darlings from throughout the year. They are always a lovely present for the Grandparents and because the sellers have a 3 for 2 offers, we keep the third one it saves me a tenner on buying a calendar. To celebrate the bright side of forgetting to do them, I invested in one of those 'Family Planner' calendars, where everyone has their own column for their appointments. Is it sad that, I am very excited, that you can also now buy a diary version too? When I was a child, I always understood family planning to be, what you did to stop you having more children than you wanted, 'the pill' and other methods. So, I have decided these calendars are quite aptly named, because I take one look at the ridiculous amount of stuff, we have to do each month with our children, and it's the best contraceptive ever!

When you are a special needs parent, mental load is somewhat enhanced. Not only do you have the every-day appointments and clubs to remember, you have to make sure you're on top of all of the other appointments, that genuinely could negatively impact your child's development if you don't attend – no pressure!

Speech and Language, Independent Living Skills, Individual Education Plan Reviews, Occupational Therapy. The list is endless, and as one support ends, another one starts. Occasionally there is a week in-between to allow you to draw breath. It feels a bit like trying to make it to a connecting flight in a foreign country where you have no idea what the airport signs mean. Depending on the individual needs of child with special needs, they may need medication. This is often frowned upon by parents not in this situation, but sometimes it is simply just necessary. Because no amount of essential oils, yoga techniques or sensory diets are going to make a significant enough difference to the life of your child. My attitude to those who do wish to judge, is that they are welcome to come and live my life for a week and we'll see if their judgement (and sanity) changes by the end of that week!

My son takes four different types of medication every day to keep his anxiety/temper under control and help his focus/concentration at school and he ensure he gets a reasonable night's sleep, which often eludes people with Autism (and their parents). When you are given a new medication CAMHS*, will give you a two-page information sheet about it, which gives you the phonetic pronunciation of the medication to avoid you making a total show of yourself in the chemist. Then there is always a brand name variation and the dosage, which of course are all totally different. My son takes 100mg of one medication and 2mg of another, so I really don't want to get those mixed up, as let's just say the consequences could be 'interesting', I like to keep him calm, not comatose!

I really don't mean to engage in a game of parenting top trumps here. But I do think it is fair to say, that parents to a child with special needs have the right to change the term to 'Mental Shitload!' The struggle is real!

*CAMHS - Child and Adolescent Mental Health Services

Outfit of The Day

Outfit of the Day has become a huge feature on social media, with bloggers, vloggers, influencers and a lot of my friends, regularly posting pictures of themselves or their children, looking fabulous, standing in the perfectly decorated 'Instagram corner' of their home, posing in their finery. Personally, I don't do it, for several reasons really:

1. I hate looking at myself in the mirror and hate posing for photographs, so why would I photograph myself in the mirror??

2. I don't have an Instagram corner in my house - all of my corners are full of cobwebs/nerf bullets/hairclips, with the skirting board in need of a good hoover and an unidentified stain on the wall.

3. My arse has gotten so round in recent years, it probably wouldn't fit in a corner, I would need a bay window instead and I never went for bay windows as I thought getting curtains for them would be too much hard work.

4. I can barely get my children to keep still long enough in the morning, to get them dressed, never mind photograph them. Generally, within 5 minutes of getting them dressed, they are covered in either crumbs/toothpaste/snot or some other unidentified stain, that I hope will wear off as the day goes on. I worry the stain will cause their teacher to think I'm a bad parent, so I don't want that level of judgement from the world of social media too!

So, I have to be honest, this O.O.T.D craze has escaped me. I do occasionally look at other people's chosen Outfit of the Day, but to be honest, I'm just not that into them. I do however love looking at people's special occasion outfits, especially the more ostentatious ones.

One of my Facebook friends, outfits and make-up belong on a Paris catwalk, she is utterly fabulous, and her posts always catch my attention, dreaming of the days before I had children when I had the spare cash to buy a rail of new dresses and the body to look good in them.. Sometimes I even screenshot her as an idea for the look I want next time I get invited to a wedding (still dreaming}. I do hope that isn't considered stalking!

My focus in this piece, however, is on a totally different kind of outfit of the day. With Christmas looming, I have succumbed to the latest seasonal retail pressure. I decided, instead of buying a chocolate advent calendar, that tastes vaguely of cardboard, I would this year treat my offspring to a treats' advent calendar. After a particularly challenging year in our household, I even managed to convince my husband that we would buy them, rather than lie to him and tell him the grandparents got them.

Saoirse being almost 13 is getting a beauty calendar, I picked one with nail varnish I like the look of, that we can 'share'. Patrick is getting an educational Lego calendar, as Lego is the only toy that has a calming effect on Patrick, this is a practical and therapeutic purchase, worthy of the price tag. My 6-year-old Erin however, is getting the LOL doll O.O.T.D calendar. One tiny plastic doll and the 24 pieces of accompanying crap, that will no doubt end up further littering all of my potential 'Instagram corners'.

Seriously who invented this shite! In an age where most us, barring a few oil magnates, are committed to vaguely trying to be environmentally conscious. LOL arrive in an orb of plastic that is 12 times their actual size, packed full with their mini accessories that would put Celine Dion to shame (she is the Imelda Marcos of the 21st century having not 3,000 pairs of shoes, but 10,000, most of which are in storage). Each accessory is carefully wrapped in layers of more, cheap, neon plastic, padding out the offending orb, to make you feel like you are getting a lot of stuff and therefore, value for money. You aren't! They are a total rip off and probably have a greater negative impact on the environment than a radioactive waste plant, no doubt doubling landfill deposits in the week following Christmas.

But who is truly at fault here? The mass marketeers of this 8cm crime against the ocean, or us, for buying them? I have to be honest I have had this battle with my conscience for the last 2 months, as every item on Erin's Santa letter is pre-fixed with the word LOL.

She and her friends all talk about them incessantly, and have the cute names of each one memorised, knowing who has the pink hair with the blue stripe, versus the blue hair with the pink strip. They do all of course come with an even more miniature, Lil' LOL (baby) and a pet, obviously teeny tiny dogs are again making a comeback as a fashion accessory. I thought we were done with all that, when Paris Hilton fell off the face of the earth.

But as Erin's obsession has reached the point of naming one of our chickens after an LOL doll, Hoops MVP, I really have to waver from my environmental commitment for just a little while, until after Santa visits. It's a battle between being, 'Mother Nature' or 'Best Mother Ever.'

I promise, that by way of compensation to the environment, in 2020, I'll only use canvas bags when shopping, and do my absolute best to actually remember to take the metal straws, I bought last year, out of my handbag whenever I buy a smoothie.

Rebel Without A Watch

Do many people actually enjoy the benefits of the clocks go back? The odd few, may be delighted with the extra hour in bed, but those with young children think, "Ah Crap an extra hour of Paw Patrol/Peppa" to fill. As a parent to a child with Autism who thrives on routine, it can be torture. Patrick doesn't really follow the clock on the wall, more his internal body clock. So, it will be weeks before he settles into the new time, meaning lots of early mornings and meltdowns before school.

It also causes me to struggle as I am a terrible time keeper, and now I'll have to double check everything to ensure the clock/watch I'm working from actually has the correct time. I know I could just check my phone, but I can never find it and my fit bit isn't always charged. I wasn't always late, so where did it all go wrong?

When I was a child, my Dad would drive me wherever I needed to go. Following a bad car accident at the age of 21 he lost all his top teeth and needed false ones, He also has bottle thickness glasses since he was a child, so he has always been very particular about getting my eyes and teeth checked regularly to ward off any optical or dental demons early on, prevention is better than cure after all. As a child I got to know all of the receptionist/assistants at any appointment really well. The reason for this, is that we always turned up at least forty minutes early to every appointment I've ever had.

When going on holidays, Dad would ensure we left for the airport roughly 5 hours ahead of the flight, to allow for bad traffic, accidents along the way, poor parking, earthquakes and tropical storms, growing up in the Wales the last two weren't very likely – but Dad's motto was 'better to be safe than sorry.'

My parents tell me that I wasn't a particularly bad or difficult teenager, I never got drunk beyond recognition, (although I was partial to sharing a bottle of peach Concorde with my other underage friends at the cricket pavilion of a Friday night), there were no dodgy boyfriends, no crazy clothes or hairstyles. My bedroom always had a post-apocalyptic feel to it and I had refined my wildly irritated and incredulous stare perfectly, but nothing out of the ordinary when it came to teenage stuff.

However, when I went off to University at the age of 18, that all changed. I got a tattoo and piercings (this was 25 years ago when it was still rebellious to do so.) I also had to repeat my second year because the first time around I spent most of my time in the pub. My biggest act of rebellion, and probably the most distressing to my Dad was that I also become very, very tardy, I was late for anything and everything.

I'm sorry to say at the age of 43 nothing has changed. I am ALWAYS late, particularly in the mornings. As a busy parent, I like to squeeze everything I can into my day, so I always find something to do to fill that spare ten minutes, unfortunately the task I pick, usually takes more like twenty minutes to complete, making me late.

My children are equally as disastrous as me to get out of the door in the morning. So, I am always chasing them into the car, with a chorus of "hurry up, did you clean your teeth? did you eat breakfast? Hurry up, just have a cereal bar" It's a well-known parenting song that you never see in nursery rhymes books. Many mornings, I'm so short of time, I have to make the choice between should I brush my hair or my teeth?!

Do you remember getting joke-books from the school book club? I loved the section of funny reasons why people hadn't got their homework:

My dog ate it! My brother farted a hole through it! What homework?

Yesterday morning I broke my record for leaving late because I couldn't find my phone. Almost every good lateness story starts with I couldn't find my...........fill in the blank, but there are lots of great excuses for tardy behaviour. I am sure lateness is something we can all identify with, so, I thought it would be fun share some of my excuses for being late, all of them genuine, I'd love to hear your own:

• I couldn't find my car keys. This happens to me often. My favourite thing about my car is that, it opens automatically if the keys are nearby, you don't have to take them out of your bag. It locks this way too, when you are 10 feet away from the car. Having a Mary Poppins style, bottomless pit of a handbag, this particular car feature is, in my opinion, Epic!! The only problem is, that despite the fact I have now had the car for over a year, every morning when I go to look for the keys, they aren't in the little box, I have dedicated to keys on the bookshelf, they still are in my bag from the day before. But do I ever remember this, do I hell, so at least twice a week, I am late because I am looking for my bloody keys.

• I got stuck behind a herd of cows/tractor. I live in Leitrim, Rural Ireland, the beautiful, but arse-end of nowhere, so this needs no further explanation! Depending on the mood of the farmer, delays can range from five to fifteen minutes.

• I ripped my top on the lock of the shed. On the day in question, I snagged my favourite black top on the rabbit shed lock, ripping it slightly. As it is my favourite black top (you know, the one ladies, it's from Penneys/Primark and only cost €8, but goes with everything and cannot be replaced as they only ever had it in one branch). I had to go back in the house to change it so I could hopefully fix it later before it ripped beyond repair. It is also one of the few tops that adequately covers my current physique, so finding a change of top took a while. Hence, I was seven minutes late leaving.

• There was a bull at my kitchen window and I couldn't leave the house. Again, as I live in Leitrim, no further explanation is needed really. But he looked very angry and I didn't fancy discussing what was bothering him, whilst running to my car.

• I couldn't get my dog to come inside. Heidi is a 17-month-old German Shepard who has a severe case of ODD, for those unfamiliar this is a new and terrifying condition, it is Oppositional Defiance Disorder. In Heidi's case, it basically means, she's a little shit who doesn't just not do as she is told, but will do the exact opposite to deliberately wind me. Trying to catch her is like cuddling a toddler smothered in olive oil.

• Laddered Tights and Hair Straighteners – this one is particularly special to me as it helped me to achieve one of my dreams. A while ago, I laddered not just one but two pairs of tights. After I finally left the house, I was suddenly struck with idea that I had left my straighteners switched on, so I just had to go home and check. They were, of course, OFF. My Whats App message chronicling the calamitous start to my day got played on Today FMs Dermot and Dave show – that's that one ticked off my bucket list. They even sent me some of their cheese and crackers socks, my life was complete – but I was still 16 minutes late in leaving.

• I've forgotten to take my meds. The final and the more serious section of this piece. For the last three years I have been taking anti-depressants. After years of fighting the need for some pharmaceutical support, I succumbed. I just need them! No explanation necessary. Without them, it is highly likely that my world would fall off its axis and there would be a catastrophic tsunami of my stress engulfing our family life. The waves are big enough already without that!

I've always been the queen of making a short story long, so I'll re-direct you back to my original point. Yesterday I was 26 minutes late leaving the house. I'd lost my phone and as we no longer have a landline (does anyone under the age of 50 have one anymore?) I couldn't phone myself to locate it. After tipping the contents of my massive, 724 pocket hand-bag on the bed, pulling out multiple drawers and up-ending the washing basket on the floor, I finally found it in my dressing gown pocket.

I then remembered that my daughter Erin was going on an away-day to another school, so the pasta I had given her was no good as she wouldn't have access to heat it up, so I had to make her a sandwich instead.

Saoirse couldn't find her school jumper, and because they are so shockingly expensive, I had only bought her one. I then had to take a few minutes out of my tight morning schedule, to lecture her on the importance of getting your stuff ready the night before - this of course never works as I don't model that behaviour myself. So, she gave me a teenage scowl and a tut.

Despite my shocking time keeping skills, Saoirse always managed a Primary School to always achieve the 'very good' score in the punctuality section of her end of year report. I can only assume it was calculated on an average of my late drop offs and the mornings my Dad took her. On my Dad's days, she needed her own key to open up the building, as no one else is there at that ridiculous hour of the morning. So, it all averaged out well.

I honestly don't know if I will ever change. Apparently as a woman, I should innately be able to multi task, maybe I'm a man, as I really cannot multi task without getting distracted and wandering off doing something else. Maybe one day I'll take my own advice and get ready the night before, but for there's always something on Netflix that us much more appealing that doing that!

Now, I need to go, has anyone seen my........

Sock Monster

I love sleeping and my weekend treat is always to have a lie in. But as he gets up early on a Saturday to train the local kids rugby team, Mick always gets the lie on a Sunday morning. I always feel aggrieved that I have to get up. Our children are of an age that they could potter around the house with us still in bed, but the animals need to be let and out fed, and Patrick likes to have someone with him whilst he is playing Minecraft in the playroom, so one of us has to get up.

In previous years I would have the internal battle every Sunday morning about going to mass. Just like a fitness class, I would come up with a raft of plausible reasons not to go, but in all honesty, I knew I should just give up and get it over with and it was never as bad I as thought it would be. More recently I have become a lapsed catholic. I try to convince myself and others it's because I am disillusioned by shocking behaviour of some members of the catholic church in past years. But whilst that is definitely a factor, it's mainly because I just can't be arsed to go.

That is of course unless it's a pre-communion or confirmation mass, then I do go, because although I am definitely a hypocrite who only does the sacraments because I like a good party afterwards, I do believe that it would be rude not at least go to the preparatory masses.

If it isn't raining too heavily, we may go for a walk down our local woods with Heidi. The kids play hide and seek, as long as they stay within 10 feet of us though to prevent abduction. I tell them every week that they are not allowed to paddle too deep in the water, they must allow at least 2 inches between the top of their wellies and the water line.

They do of course always ignore me and end up with soaking wet feet and whinge the whole way back to the car about it! Why do think I bloody told you not to do it in the first place!

By the time we've got home, mopped the floor of their wet foot prints, and put the clothes they've worn for less than an hour into the wash, it is early afternoon and the Sunday afternoon doom begins to set in. I'm like a child who hasn't done their homework, dreading the return to school on Monday morning.

Although I should relish Sunday quiet time, for some reason I just become really irritable and likely to start world war three in rural Ireland because I'm so stroppy with my poor husband. We've been together for sixteen years, so he's learnt to give me a wide birth and stay in the sitting room watching sport.

Maybe scaling the mountain of washing that needs to be put away is the reason for my dour face. I am so busy during the week; often looking at something interesting on my phone, so I rarely get the opportunity to put washing away. It sits on the top of the chest freezer in the utility room, making it harder and harder to lift the lid as each day passes.

On a Sunday it gets transported to our bed, where it is

sorted into to neat little piles ready to be re-located to each individual bedroom or cupboard.

I gave up ironing most things after my third child started school, so everything gets a good shake and neat fold in an effort to mask my poor housewifery skills. If I am lucky, Patrick is in a good mood and won't come into the room and flip over all of my neat little piles, because he knows it's an easy way to provoke a reaction from me, and oh how he loves to get a reaction! I always leave the socks until last. Sock sorting can take a good hour. Socks of course never match up, Mick rolls his socks together when putting them in the wash, to make sure they stay in pairs, he thinks he's smart. But they never dry properly in the tumble dryer and have to be separated to dry on the radiator, which is exactly where they will stay for another week blocking heat and going crispy. I did buy a little basket for lonely odd socks to hang out, until they were re-united with their partner. I don't why I thought storing them in their own little basket instead of in the communal 'to be put away' basket, would warm my feelings towards them, but I decided it would.

It didn't!

They just sat there for weeks until finally, I decided to bin them, only to, of course, find their long-lost buddy the following day.

Last year I decided I was going to stop buying patterned socks and just buy single colour socks, because they could be easily matched with one another.

Genius!

I didn't however manage to predict that sorting socks the same colour, but different sizes, would cause me even more irritation. So now I stand there measuring them all against each other, and surprise, surprise I never seem to be able to find a match with them either. What the flip was I thinking?! There really are no short cuts when it comes to sorting socks, we just have to accept that where it is, they hide from week to week, will always be one of life's great mysteries.

On the plus side, I do step from side to side whilst sock sorting, as this a great way to get to my 10,000 steps. Every now and again I throw in a little squat to help toward achieving my goal of a bikini body. Obviously the 'after', not the 'before' shot you see on the cover of 'Closer' magazine. I always feel a little flutter of joy when I get to the last pair of socks, I carefully unfurl them just like savouring the unwrapping of that stray Ferrero Rocher you found at the back of the sweet cupboard the first Thursday after New Year's Day. But wait, what is that? SAND! Stuck in a sock after last week's trip to the woods.

All over the bed, all over the clean, neatly piled socks.

For Fucks Sake!!!

I give up.

I head to the kitchen and slice tiny slivers of ice-cream off either end of the Vienetta we have for Sunday dessert and just hope no one will notice!

Sunday Bloody Sunday!!!

I've Started So I'll Finish

After the serious upset of a house falling through, followed by 6 months of searching in every county bordering Leitrim to find 'mi casa', Mick and I finally agreed on building a house. The site we bought already had full planning permission for a house we liked the look of, so it was the perfect option.

Living in Leitrim we were able to build a 2,000sq foot house on acre of land for much the same price you would pay for a sun-room in Dublin. I was never madly house proud, but I invested lots of our hard-earned cash into knick-knacks and storage solutions to make the house look pretty.

I did of course forget to budget for a cleaner to dust all this shite!

When Saoirse and Patrick were small, I bought one of these cute little signs that say:

Excuse the mess

our children are making memories.

Within a year, whilst trying to make his sister remember not to play with his trucks, Patrick threw the sign at her and it smashed to pieces. Probably not a bad thing as the only memories they will have are of me regularly screaming like a fish wife that "I'm sick of this, the place is a pig sty, I'm putting everything in the bin!" I have now moved on to a much better sign, which says:

Excuse the mess,

we live here!

Although I gave up my paid part time job earlier this year, to stay at home, as a Mum and as carer to Patrick, I now consider that to be a full-time job, without being a cleaner too.

I put more diesel in my car now, than I ever did travelling 120km round trip to work in Sligo, three times a week. As I am now chaperone and driver for every appointment and social club my children attend each week, which goes into double figures between the three of them.

Leitrim is the only county where land is sold by the gallon, our beautiful acre of land has now become a swamp that Heidi, the dog loves, to run around in and then re-decorate my house with. My children never put stuff away and I never act on my threats of never buying another toy, t-shirt or bag of crisps ever again if they won't clean up. It is true, modern day life does not support a tidy house and I certainly cannot afford a cleaner and even if I could, Mick would not agree to it. I cannot complain too much about my children being the source of clutter of chaos we live in, because I certainly don't lead by example.

Every few weeks, I suddenly become the Wild Woman of Borneo and stomp around the house chastising anyone in view, telling them if we don't get a handle on the mess then I will go mad(der). I then make a valiant effort to reorganise every cupboard, drawer and basket we own, filling twenty bin bags to be deposited in various different locations, re-cycling bank, skip and charity shop.

One of the biggest problems is that I actually used to manage a charity shop and 75% of our current clutter has been purchased in there. Because, obviously it was too much of a bargain to leave behind. Mick warned me every week, no more crap. It's not a bargain if we don't need it, but every week I sneak the bags in past his rolling eyes.

Those valiant efforts always start with such vigour and vim they would likely to win my village a tidy towns gold medal. But they quickly fizzle out as soon as something distracts me.

Apparently, Autism and ADHD are genetic, and there are no doubt Patrick's attention span challenges come from me. I have the attention span of a newt. The slightest thing will throw me off task, old photos in a drawer, a funny video in a Whats App message (and the forty replies that follow), organising the kids summer clothes, even though its January! I am a total disaster!

To give you a supreme example, I cleaned Mick's car a few weeks ago, and every day I chastise myself as I walk past the car mats that I took out to hoover. I never actually hoovered them, but they are now sitting outside on the un-returned plastic chairs we borrowed from our neighbours two years ago, waiting to be put back into the car. That task is constantly delayed by the fact they get more and more saturated with each passing rainy Leitrim day.

So, in truth, the phrase "I've started so I'll finish" only ever applies to me, if we're talking about a packet of chocolate hobnobs.

I came across a new sign recently that actually does suit my home perfectly:

Excuse the mess, but my children are feral little creatures and I've lost the will to give a shit!

Sadly, I'm not brave enough to put it up - the truth hurts.

Erectile Dysfunction

When we moved into our new house in 2005, my Mother in Law, Kathleen and her friend Alan came down to help us move in. Kathleen helped me to unpack and unwrap all of the crockery, ornaments and vaguely valuable possessions. and Mick and Alan got busy drilling.

I'm sorry if those outdated gender roles offend anyone, but that's just the way it was that day.

I can barely operate the blender so there's no way I'm going to trust myself operating a drill.

Alan insisted on putting up the curtain poles and went about it with military style precision measuring for the drop of the curtains etc. I'm not sure where exactly he went wrong, maybe the numbers on the tape measure were in a foreign language, maybe it's because our house is slightly elevated spot, but every set of bloody curtains ending up being a good 5 inches off the floor – not the look I was going for.

At this point, I realised erectile dysfunction was clearly an issue for older men. I politely thanked him for all of his hard work, through gritted teeth whilst silently wishing I could poke his eyes out with the drill.

You may think that's a bit extreme but it was my new home and I actually cared what it looked like back in those days – -having spent half my budget on glossy magazines, I had an interior design vision!

I took a deep breath and thought it was no great harm as we could change them as soon as Kathleen and Alan were back on the road to Dublin.

But as this was a newly built house, with newly plastered and painted walls, Mick flat out refused to take the curtain poles down and start again as it would leave great big gaping holes in the walls. For several years, I had to suffer the torture of looking at these half-mast curtains every day. Imagine the lad at school that suddenly grew 5 inches one weekend and his Mum refused to buy him new school trousers exposing his white, hairy ankles, to me that is how the curtain gap looked.

This may not seem like a huge deal to many of you, but I have mild OCD, so much so that my friend used to re-arrange my photo frames on my mantlepiece every time she visited as they were "too symmetrical". I would sit on the sofa watching TV at night being taunted by the Wicklow gap at the base of the curtains, making my skin crawl, much like a huge spider scurrying away in the house of an arachnophobe would.

Whilst Mick was not the perpetrator of this crime against interior design, as the years passed I began to learn that this was actually just a 'man thing' as whenever I asked him or my Dad to put up nails for shelves, photo-frames, paintings etc. they were never just quite how I wanted them and I had to accept that erectile dysfunction is indeed universal.

Nothing on Pinterest is ever wonky, or slightly too high. I'm guessing they have carpenters, professionally trained in dealing with complicated erections, working on those picture-perfect images. As the vast majority of us mere mortals, don't have a home makeover team on speed dial or even a handyman that returns answer phone messages, living within a 50-mile radius, then we are stuck relying on the free labour of the nearest, erectily dysfunctional man, with a tool obsession. I guess beggars can't be choosers really. I have had to learn to accept a few things about my husband (and men in general.).

One being that, they cannot read minds, especially women's.

They do not understand the intricacies of our plan, our vision, our creative genius and when we showed them a picture of it in a magazine, despite telling us otherwise, they were not actually paying attention.

Mick has always joked, the only set of instructions he has ever seen me read, were those in a pregnancy test, whereas he, of course reads and follows instructions to the letter, so maybe I should start typing out my instructions with a diagram. when I want pictures put up in a specific spot, with lines pointing out to which part of the wall each edge of the frame is meant to rest. This may indeed be the cure for erectile dysfunction.

I have resigned myself to the fact that, as I cannot operate a drill safely or a screwdriver accurately, it is best just to smile sweetly at the slightly wonky shelf and say ' that's perfect dear' otherwise I will be subject to the true meaning of DIY, when he throws his tools to floor shouting "if you don't like it, you can bloody well "Do It Yourself".

After 14 years of a happy marriage I have learnt that there are sometimes that I just have to keep quiet. Mick never takes kindly to me criticising his driving, his parking, his sports team and I decided that us women just have to accept our nails will forever be wonky, but then maybe I'll just give that carpenter one last call…

A Form of Torture

Whenever I'm applying for a new passport, I always get 2 forms in the post office, just in case I make a mistake on the first one. Of course, I always do make a mistake, usually almost always at the end of the form. It's incredibly frustrating and may cause a few cheeky little profanities to slide effortlessly out of my mouth.

I hate filling in forms! It's a task that requires military style planning, what colour pen should I use? It must be a non-smudgy pen that my hand won't squish onto a spider scrawl, when I fill out the columns on the right-hand side of the page. Are block capitals needed? If so, does that lower-case e actually look like a capital E, after I tried to correct it when I forgot about block capitals, half way through filling in the form? Is it a noticeable enough infringement for the paperwork police to mercilessly reject my form, sending it back to me with a snotty letter referring me to the guidelines of how to fill in a fecking form.

You can almost sense the tut, the eye roll and the mutterings of the office administrator going "FFS it isn't rocket science." Even worse a bright yellow sticker on the envelope, informing me of my crime against form filling!! Oh, the shame!

When you are a special needs parent, the forms are endless. They are needed in duplicate, triplicate and whatever comes after that, is it quadlicate? Spellcheck is telling me no, but I'm going to stick with the naming approach of multiple babies for multiple forms.

You have to fill in a form for absolutely bloody everything, healthcare, education support, equipment, benefits, medication, your wine allowance – which I would like to point out should be increased with every sodding form you have to complete! Some of the forms are incredibly serious, deciding if your child does one of hundred behaviours never /sometimes/regularly/constantly, could be the decision that swings the dial to whether your child receives a diagnosis or not.

Whilst those of you who don't have experience in this field may think, well surely you don't want a diagnosis? Honestly, the diagnosis process is as long and complicated as a Games of Thrones book. So, when you get to this point, you almost greet a diagnosis with relief, because it is the key that (supposedly) unlocks to the door to all of the supports you so desperately need.

It's not sufficient to fill in just one form, and one of the quadlicates get passed to the relevant services. No, that would be simple and when did anyone favour simplicity over bureaucracy, that just isn't the done thing in polite society! I sat in a meeting with Autism Services last year and flawlessly reeled off everything that had happened with Patrick for the previous 5 years. I was quite literally like the parent of a new-born and knew every fart, burp and smile that had occurred in graphic detail (times, dates, people attended, grammatical errors - the works).

The Autism Services Specialist commented how

detailed my response was, I faked a smile and told her I had a good memory for detail, forcing down the urge to shout, "that's because I've repeated it so making freaking times!" It continues, ad infinitum. The more challenges your child presents with, the more forms you have to fill in.

When you get to the Psychologist stage for your child (and also for yourself if your child's behaviour is particularly challenging), you not only have to fill in forms about what happened, but also what should have happened, what could have happened if you handled it differently and how you felt about what happened. Am I being awkward or does it seem excessive to have thoughts about your thoughts? It's like working for an American corporate where you fill your day by having meetings about meetings.

The forms aren't even phrased in a way that anyone actually speaks and you have to open your thesaurus to fill in the form in, in such a way that the Psychologist may think you are reasonably intelligent, thoughtful and bothered.

The only problem is, that half the time, after dealing with an epic meltdown (from either yourself or your child) then the last thing you feel like doing is filling in a form about it, you can't write and hold an extra-large glass of wine at the same time. So, half the time, you end up filling in the form from memory, an hour before your appointment, obviously using three different pens, and changing your handwriting slightly each time so they don't know! I didn't do my forms last weekend as my son's meltdowns were so utterly draining, that in all honesty, I didn't have the energy (aka I really couldn't be arsed, I just wanted to stare zombie-like at Netflix and eat chocolate covered anything (chocolate smudges on the form is a huge no no!)

I defiantly told my Psychologist on the Monday morning, that I just didn't do my homework! I felt liberated, I felt 16 again. It was akin to telling my smart-arse English teacher, the poem, he gave us by T.S Eliot was crap and it was apt that T.S Eliot was an anagram of toilets, because the poem belonged in one. I was cool, I was tough, I was a REBEL!

Unlike my English teacher, who gave me detention for a week, the Psychologist was very understanding and worked through my feelings capably with me. Where's the fun in that! I wanted to be a therapy rebel! A grown-up wobbler isn't rebellious when it's met with a kind an understanding response!!

In order for it to be effective you have to be totally honest with the forms. Because the paperwork police know everything, even if you only cleaned your teeth for less than a minute this morning.

I am by nature very honest in my communication, but the information you have to share would set the nose of the most stringent civil liberties advocate into overdrive. The United States' Patriot act could learn a thing or two from the SEN paperwork police.

In short, I feeling that form filling, should be added to the United Nations list of cruel and unusual punishments. It's just torture.

Smells Like Teen Spirit

My eldest child, Saoirse has just entered the black hole of being a 'teenager'. She has always been our textbook child, she met all of her milestones as expected, has never struggled at school, has never been in trouble, is a joy to be around. Blah blah blah. If daughters were Facebook posts, Saoirse would be that annoying picture-perfect post, that looks like it was copy and pasted from Pinterest.

But just like it says in the parenting textbooks, with her 13th birthday in the bag, she is stepping out of Pinterest corner and into the messy world of teen tutting and tantrums. She has become a new, often unrecognisable person, especially since starting secondary school earlier this year.

I had been warned that teenage girls, usually stop speaking to from about the age of 13 to 16. I had been pretty devastated by this idea, but now the way things are going, I think it might be for the best.

I can honestly say, I am 'so over' the teenage years already and she isn't actually 13 for a few weeks yet. So, what is it that is causing me such despair? I had to say in a poem:

Saoirse

Although she's only just become a teen,

There is a now a demon where my little girl had been.

Every time I speak, she rolls her eyes,

If I say it something wrong, she runs and cries.

Her skin is starting to get a little spotty,

And her moods and whims are driving me dotty.

Her phone seems to be glued to her hand,

She wants expensive clothes with a fancy brand.

She's never tired and likes to stay up late.

But getting her out of bed, I really do hate.

To her brother and sister, she's always mean,

The floor to her room can no longer be seen.

Mugs, books and bottles I always miss,

As they lay under her bed, lost in the Abyss.

Her hair I wish she'd brush or wash,

She's only nice when she wants some dosh.

She seems to think I was never a teen,

"For God's sake mum, you don't know what I mean!"

With her friends she'll happily giggle and whisper,

Preferring to scream and shout at us or her sister.

She simply has to be always right,

Telling us this with all of her might.

The door to her room is always locked,

My number on her phone will soon be blocked.

We're about to start with Kardashian Brows,

And lipstick pouts that look like sows'

There'll be no going out with her skirt up her ass!

I do hope that phase will quickly pass.

Maybe the next 3 years will soon fly by,

And speak to her, again we'll try.

Until then I'll pick my battles through gritted teeth,

Remembering my gorgeous Saoirse is underneath.

So, I'll make sure to hold on tight for dear life,

Smiling on through the trouble and strife,

And soon enough a young woman will emerge.

As my love and pride continue to surge.

Happy 13th Birthday Saoirse!

This is dedicated to the parents, teachers and all who interact with teenagers regularly.

May the odds be forever in your favour.

The struggle is real!

Part Four

Going South

Faye's Anatomy

I've never been mistaken for a supermodel, but back when I was younger, I did get told I looked like Kelly McGillis (The Flying Instructor in Top Gun).

At the age of fifteen, I was 5 foot 7, a size 8 with long blonde hair and had curves in all the right places, so I was quite well liked among the fickle boys. Then, at the age of sixteen, I got told that my knees where knackered from playing too much netball. I played five or six times a week, so my poor old knees had just had enough. I had to stop immediately or potentially be wheelchair bound by the time I was forty. Stopping playing that much sport every week, was the start of my long and ongoing battle with my weight. Although I grew 3 inches taller, I grew many more inches wider too. By the time I was eighteen I was a size 16 and pretty unhappy.

After being called a nasty name at my eighteenth birthday party, I decided to diet and lost over 30lbs and 2 dress sizes. I then spent my college years between the pub and the gym, with an occasional lecture thrown in to keep me from being expelled.

I managed to keep the weight off through college, but after a summer working in America and eating grilled cheese sandwiches and Tootsie Rolls, my weight starting creeping back on. As every bit of me expanded my boobs became very competitive and developed more cups that a charity coffee morning.

I always kid myself that I was thin for years, but in

reality, I have only spent roughly 3 years of my adult life with a BMI below the holy grail of 25. My varying waistline has caused me considerable stress over the years and I have tried every diet under the sun. I did a torturous six-week detox before my wedding and lost 20lbs, only to have put half of it back on by the end of the first dance. I was then devastated when, at 35 weeks pregnant with Saoirse, my GP felt my stomach and told me "there's a lot more of you than there is baby." I was not however devastated enough, to stop eating for triplets.

Despite trying so many different diets over the years, Slimming World, Sugar Free, C9 Aloe Vera, I never manage to keep the weight off. This is the story of billions of women and is what keeps the diet industry alive and thriving. With not only the slimmer's waistlines growing, but the multi-billion-dollar bank balances of the diet companies too. I know the magic formula for maintaining a healthy weight is really very simple; 'eat less, move more' The theory may be simple but the practical most certainly is not.

I've gained most of my weight in the last 3 years. I kid myself that it because of the medication I take and whilst that probably does have some impact, it's more likely the way I self-medicate that is the biggest factor. Chocolate is my drug of choice; I would eat Nutella off a spoon!

My friend recently bought me some of those Butlers Hot Chocolate pieces, but did I enjoy family time making them with my children? Nope, I enjoyed me time, by eating them whole as if they were a box of chocolates. I am a regular user and as I am a stress/comfort eater, it is fair to say, Autism made me fat(ter). I have heard people say that sugar is more addictive than cocaine. Detoxing from sugar is beyond vicious.

The last time I did it, I experienced flu-like symptoms for three full weeks. My negative body image led me to actually feel delighted, when I recently got diagnosed with an under active thyroid. Because, although I was still fat, at least I had a genuine medical reason for it.

The biggest challenge in my anatomy is without a doubt my boobs. I was doomed from the start. My Nana always had what she called "bosoms" and was well endowed in that area. My poor Mum, despite being 5 feet 2 wears a J cup bra, her boobs walk into a room five minutes before she does.

I know we should promote positive body image, especially around young girls and to be fair I do try. I never complain about my weight or size in front of my children or others, and I stopped buying magazines when Saoirse was a toddler as I didn't want her to get into the idea of what the so-called 'perfect' body looks like. But I do want to be healthy, so my new fit-bit is fully charged and raring to go, now if only my metabolism would feel the same, but having recently discovered the low-carb keto diet, I'm hoping to be a size 10 by Christmas! Or at least fit into the, two sizes too small, overpriced dress I bought for my husband's work Ball! I'll bloody have to or I won't be going as everything else in my wardrobe is at least 2 sizes too small as well!

Someone pass me the Spanx!

*At the time of going to press, I am not a size 10, but I can zip up the dress for the ball!

Breast is Best

Most mornings when I wake up, I'm not actually sure if I am lying on my back or my front. Most women could tell this based on the position of their breasts but with mine, I really cannot be sure. They could be anywhere, as they are so big and unruly, they move around a lot in the transit of sleep, being unbridled and free to roam.

Although, it's probably good they are free to move, otherwise if I slept on my front, I could scare my family every morning, looking like I was levitating a few feet off the bed. It is no secret amongst my friends, that I absolutely hate my boobs and if a genie were to appear before me, a nice little storm in a C cup would be my very first wish. In my teens and twenties, they were a nice, reasonably manageable size, that were pert beacons of womanhood.

Whilst I was never able to go braless, I could certainly still stop in the pretty section in Marks and Spencer and not have to search for a home for them in Millets tent section. They were often stared at in conversations with men, who hadn't yet received the news that women don't actually like it when you do that.

They were definitely on the larger side, with one middle aged letch, telling me "you don't get many of them to the pound love" trying to cop a feel. Needless to say, the only feel he copped, was the inside of my right hand across his face. I think he genuinely believed he was "only being nice!"

As I got into my thirties, they became functional,

delivering breakfast, lunch and dinner to each of my new-borns. I am firmly in the 'Breast is Best' camp when it comes to feeding small babies, and I really wish more was done in Ireland to encourage women to do it. It's often touted that formula is nearly is good as breast milk, but no actually it isn't, and we should stop trying to pretend that it is. I do respect every woman's right to make that decision for herself. I'm not dreamy and romantic about it in any way and when sharing my experience with expectant Mum's, I tell the truth, whilst it is lovely to connect with your baby and it gives them all the antibodies etc. they need, it is also exhausting and pretty boring to sit for 45 minutes, several times every day whilst your child messes with its dinner.

It also, isn't always easy. Every one of my children were barely off the boob for the first 3 days until my milk came in. For someone as impatient and as results driven as me, that can be pretty bloody frustrating and coupled with post-natal hormones, it can be verging on catastrophic.

But I have never regretted doing it, even though the first time Mick's older brother walked into the room when I was feeding, was an experience I could have lived without. Also, the time I stood chatting to my friend's husband, not realising I had forgotten my breast pads and had 2 perfectly circular milky targets on my brown cotton blouse. Any one for darts?!

I quickly learned how to discreetly let them loose in public, like juggling a liquid filled basketball under a blanket, whist also holding on to a 15lb piece of slippery ice, easy-peasy! I am very proud of myself, that I did it for six months, although all of my children were combination fed on boob and bottle from between 8-14 weeks, I'm not a saint! I have to be honest, I do find it a little strange when women are still breastfeeding their toddlers, having experienced feeding Erin with 4 teeth, it is torture and I personally feel as soon as they hit 6 months and teeth start to appear, that is more than enough for me.

But as with choosing bottle over breast, choosing when to stop feeding is a personal choice every woman should be allowed to make without judgement, comment, rolling eyes or yuk faces.

Whilst breastfeeding is wonderful for helping you lose your baby weight; it is not so kind to the level of elasticity in your boobies. Feeding three babies for a combined total of 18 months, coupled with, my advancing years and ever-increasing scales reading, my boobs have somewhat gotten out of control.

 Like a child with ADHD, it is impossible to keep them still when you want them to, and they could burst out of your top, swimsuit or even bra if they are not tutored in the right way. Unlike children with ADHD, you are at least allowed to strap them down in an effort to keep them under control, and my, over the shoulder boulder holders, have become bigger and more matronly the more unruly my boobs have become. If I carry on the way I am going, in a few years, I will be able to touch my toes with my nipples.

This is not the 'fabulous at fifty' look I had in mind, so

my name is now slowly moving up the waiting list for a breast reduction operation because, they do in fact cause me a lot of back pain.

I could have them reduced on my health insurance but you not only need for that you need the holy trinity of, a letter from your osteopath, a minimum of G cup and a BMI of 25.

If I had a BMI of 25, I'm sure I would end up needing a nose job too, after falling flat on my face, being pulled down by the force of grav-titty.

Changing My Religion

My eldest daughter has recently started secondary school. As society is now progressing, and the school is non-denominational, they are learning about various religions. She keeps educating me about Islam, Buddhism and Hinduism.

Not long after she started her new journey, I embarked on one of my own and changed my religion, to Keto! Keto? But isn't that a diet, the one where "your body eats itself?" I often get asked. Well no, there's A LOT more to it than that, the first thing to remember is that it does require the unyielding dedication of any religion. You must have faith in the fact that the great God ketosis will turn your fat into an energy source as long as you shun the devil of carbs. Well not all carbs, 'clean carbs' are ok, just as long as they don't exceed 20g a day of course. If you give your blind faith to ketosis then, just like when you receive the Catholic Eucharist, your body will be transformed!

When preparing for my wedding, I did the Atkins diet 2 weeks before every dress fitting. Eating bacon eggs for almost every meal didn't seem like a huge hardship to drop 10lbs in 10 days. I was a lot more sensible before the real dress fitting and did a six-week detox, dropping 20lbs in 6 weeks, to slide rather than struggle into my wedding dress.

I felt great but, sadly put on everything I lost and then some, on my food and drink fuelled honeymoon. What can I say, Canadians are great cooks! Since my 40th birthday, I have gained 50lbs. Mainly due to the fact that I am an emotional eater who eats for comfort, and as life in recent years has been difficult, I have always sought solace in Double Decker's and Dorritos.

I have sadly learnt the hard way, that despite being tiny, Aldi cookery chocolate chips have the same number of calories as normal chocolate and, despite my best efforts to locate them, the answers to life's problems cannot actually be found on the back of a golden ticket wrapped around an XL bar of chocolate. For a while, I ignored my weight, having an acceptable reason to be fat, due to an under active thyroid. But that didn't actually make me any thinner, so as my acceptance abated, I did begin to start thinking I need to do something drastic about this.

My friend had been raving about the Keto diet for the past year, and pressing me to watch Netflix program, 'The Magic Pill'. I finally got around to it, and although it was certainly convincing it didn't give me quite the kick in the ass I needed to actually start Keto, to be fair it is a very big ass, so the kick would need to be that of a rugby number 10, although I must say, Johnny Sexton is welcome to kick my ass anytime.

What did get me started, was after attending a nutrition talk at a local, 'Get Healthy' event. I hadn't even meant to go to the talk, I just wandered into the room looking for one or any of my wayward children, who kept disappearing. My friend was in there, so I decided to stay. It was, to be fair a great place to hide from the afore-mention wayward children, my husband was in the building so I was confident they wouldn't be left free to wreak to havoc that might cost me a fortune. The nutritionist didn't tell me anything I hadn't heard before.

At the end of the session, eager to get an extra five minutes away from my darling offspring. I decided I might as well ask about Keto, expecting the Nutritionist to tell me it was really bad and avoid it like the plague, I was looking for professional advice NOT to start it. It was not forthcoming!

The Nutritionist waxed lyrical about Keto, proclaiming it to be the only eating plan that has ever worked for him in his most intensive training. As a world champion Muy Thai Boxer, I couldn't really argue with his input. However, my interest, still hadn't reached the point of inspiration. Then I saw his boxing demonstration, I was inspired! Not because of his levels of fitness but because of his thighs. Don't get me wrong, I didn't fancy his thighs, I coveted his them, I wanted to get me a pair!!

The very next day, I took myself shopping for all thing's low carb, high fat. They are the 2 staples of the Keto diet, there was me thinking that it was a simple as that. How wrong could I be. My Keto friend got me onto the Keto UK Community on Facebook (the Irish page is a lot more chilled) and that is when I realised, I was entering what feels like a religion.

Don't get me wrong, it's Keto not Waco, it's not quite a cult. But it is without doubt, a way of eating that can become obsessive. Keto rule number 1 - this is not a diet. It's a way of eating, a life-long commitment on a new path of nutritional enlightenment.

Whilst although I am mildly mocking it, it really is a totally new way of eating. For years I have started my diet every Monday, gaining 3lb every Sunday night by cleaning out of the junk in my cupboards, shovelling it directly into by ever expanding belly. Most diets I attempted, rarely last passed Thursday!

I am now 9 weeks into Keto, and it's been a tough few weeks in my personal life, not the Keto, the Kiddo. Normally I would be reaching for the Nutella and my favourite spoon at this stage, but no. The way Keto works takes several days to reach a state of ketosis, meaning that it takes several days to even start working, so if you cheat, you go right back to the beginning A bit like that nasty snake at square 99 of snakes and ladders that brings you right back to square one. No chance, I like to win!! Although I did have a slight wobble, when I lost just 1kg in the first 4 weeks, I climbed back on the wagon, and stopped cheating, then lost 5kg the following week!   My Keto enlightenment is continuing. Instead of memorising the names of the patron saint of everything, you have to know the brand or alternate name of every dodgy sweetener ever invented – a number that is heading towards triple digits.   Ingesting one these evil sweeteners could result in the 20g daily carb target being passed and that is indeed sacrilege.

Like any good religion, Keto has its own deity's. Facebook is strewn with many before and after photos of people who now sport supermodel figures, having lost 3 stone since half past three on Wednesday, by managing their macros and eating grass fed butter only and drinking BPC (bulletproof coffee). Ok, I'm over exaggerating a bit, but I did see one post where a woman had lost 19lb in ten days, FFS, did she give birth to twins? Apparently not, just substituted spag-bol for spiralised courgettes.

If I am being honest, I am totally jealous!! Personally, I do 'lazy' or 'dirty' Keto, I really cannot be bothered to weight out my macros, I simply track my net carbs and make sure I keep them below the 20g mark. I am however dedicated.

The bible has been translated into over 3,000 languages. Keto can yield that many books in just a basic google search, it is everywhere. Much like the bible, there are many strange words that need a lot of explaining. Macros, Electrolytes, Fat Adaptation, powerhouse proteins, the list goes on.

New Testament Keto worshipers go very 21st century and use acronyms instead, OMAD, IF, BPC, and BMR. It all leaves me thinking WTF! I am having a slight crisis of faith though. I love Keto. Keto makes me feel good about myself. It has cured me of hunger, of afternoon naps and has given me finger nails of steel. But I'm more than a little bit exhausted by the rules, and I absolutely refuse to pee on a piece of paper to see if it's pink enough to define my day being happy or not, by telling me that I am 'in ketosis' or not. Yes, that truly is a thing!

I love one lady on Facebook, who keeps posting about

know she lost five stone, without counting a single macro and drank alcohol most nights. She is the Mary Magdalene of Keto, I love a good rebel and she is my personal role model, having uncovered Kylie-esque cheekbones underneath a previously bloated carb face.

Keto is great and if you want to be an extremist, then I absolutely respect your right to (intermittently) fast like it's Ramadan and to have a weighing scales in every room I certainly make the sign of the cross every time I step on to mine.

But personally, I like to get down and dirty, 'dirty Keto' that is, sadly for my poor husband, it's nothing more exciting than that. Now, someone pass me the Double Cream dipped Halloumi slices and a zero-carb vodka and tonic, (slimline of course!)

Hair Peace

Continuing with the image theme, I have taken some time to reflect on another cause of consternation in my life. Hair!

Earlier this year, I foolishly trusted Mick to take Patrick to the Barbers for his regular trim.

He returned an hour later, with a dramatic newly skinned animal look! Needless to say, with only a month of growing time before Saoirse making her Confirmation and a raft of Family photographs for posterity and more importantly Social Media to be taken, I was unimpressed. Hair has always managed to cause me great stress. I have that annoying fine hair that won't stay put for 5 minutes, even with the best blow dry in the world.

For most of my life, I have been blonde. Naturally or otherwise. I had a little experimentation with dark hair in my twenties, but it lasted less than a year. Last year after struggling to get the exact blonde I wanted, and the constant reappearance of my roots. I decided, I was going dark.

I was impressed with how brave I was. At the start it went way too dark, my poor hairdresser tried to hide the panic in her voice as she tried to convince me it was actually very dark brown and not full on black. I was going for dairy milk but I'd come out 70% cocoa! She toned it down a few days later and it was closer to what I was looking for. After a few weeks, I thought I'd be 'on trend' and get some balayage.

My hairdresser obliged, but warned me that it would be bad for my hair, but I was determined and she knows better than to try and change my mind. She was right! The blonde balayage destroyed it and it was like straw, I had to stay away from the field in case the donkey tried to take a chunk out of my head.

I told my hairdresser to just "cut it off', a phrase I rarely utter. Not short-short, but a short bob. Leaving me with distinct look of Mary Lou McDonald (leader of the Sinn Fein Party in Ireland.) How did that happen when I showed a picture of Scarlet Johansson????

I do actually feel sorry for hairdressers, we invest so much hope in them transforming us from head to toe. I always expect them to trim away 30lb along with my split ends and feel let down when they don't. I have to remind myself; they went to hairdressing college not Hogwarts. But outside of the professional control of the hairdresser, who are trained in the black art of blow drying, we all have battles with our hair, so I decided to write a little ditty to reflect our struggles:

Hair Today

How I wish my hair would nicely sit.

Even just for a little bit.

It's fine, fuzzy and always flyaway.

It drives me crazy every day.

My friend's hair is glossy and thick,

looking at it makes me sick.

Why can't I ever master the dry,

instead of feeling like I want to cry.

Straighteners only work for 15 mins,

and then I'm subjected to stranger's grins.

Because my hair is standing up tall,

and my stylist I need to call.

Wax, mousse, and conditioner spray,

I invest a fortune every day.

But nothing ever seems to work,

I look like a woman who's gone berserk,

If it isn't sticking out and looking scary,

it looks as flat as the wings of a fairy.

Why is my hair just never right?

When I want to look like dynamite.

I have albums of pictures with styles I love,

Black as coal or white as a dove.

But I never come out looking like that

I'm always more like a tabby cat.

My hair's so porous the colour goes funny

Especially if the weather is sunny.

Why don't I look like the picture I bring in?

Tall and lean and looking thin.

It's one of life's huge frustrations,

Like chipping nails and overdue gestations.

I really just need to learn to accept.

I'll always look wild and windswept

It's all part of my personal style.

So, I suck it up and have to smile.

Now I wonder can my hairdresser make me look like Heidi Klum next time…although it's more likely I'll end up looking my German Shepherd Heidi.

Part Six

Finding a Good Bra

The Girls of SATC

My favourite TV programme has always been Sex and The City (SATC). My best ever Christmas present was the signed photos of Sarah Jessica Parker, Mick bought me many years ago. Just like any super fan, even at the tender age of 43, they are still stuck up in my wardrobe. The most important part of the show is the friendship of the four women. I could not have got through the ten-year challenge I have experienced without my friends.

Carrie – My best friend Christine, and after a very giggly road trip she took on the nickname Lily. I don't really use the nickname much, but that is how she is stored in my phone and Lily is also one Erin's middle names, after my beloved bestie. She was also specially selected to be Patrick's Godmother; this is the biggest honour I can ever offer any of my friends.

Christine is really tall, nearly six foot in fact. To match her towering height, she also has a big personality and, just like Carrie Bradshaw, everyone is drawn to her. Not only does she fulfil all of my emotional needs, she fulfils my style needs too. We are both a similar size, and regularly steal each other's clothes! Very important in any best friend relationship!

Sadly, in 2014 Christine's beloved husband John passed away, 10 weeks after his diagnosis of oesophageal cancer. Without meaning too sound cheesy and sentimental, Christine is one my heroes. She handled this tragic blow dealt to her with such strength and dignity.

She has always simply got on with dealing with this tragic part of her life and she never lost sight of what was most important, their two little boys Seán and Oisin. She is an amazing friend and an amazing Mum. Through everything she has endured, she has never failed to lose her sparkle, and being the magpie that I am, I always want to be close to her. We have been there every step of the way for each other as we have faced the toughest challenges in our lives. I love her dearly and as the fridge magnet I bought for her says "If we live to be 103, best friends we will always be."

Charlotte - I went to see the movie Mary Poppins earlier this year, and I couldn't fail to see the similarities between Mary and my good friend Nicola. Nicola is the sensible one of my friendship group and is a quite stern. If I'm honest, I'm a little bit afraid of her and always try my best to do as I'm told!

She buys good shoes, a good coat and a good bag and always knows the right thing to do. She is the friend I go to when I need good advice. You know the kind you really don't want to hear, but you just know is right!

She's the one that never lets me buy another dress, to add to my collection that are two sizes too small, because convince myself that I will fit into for an upcoming event later that year. She also tried to tell me that getting Heidi the dog was a bad idea, dear God, why didn't I listen to her?

Just like Mary Poppins, in her bag of tricks Nicola has

all sorts of amazing stories and adventures you just never guessed were in there. She'll often shock me, by starting conversations with phrases like "when I was canoeing down the Zambezi………." She had an adventurous life before getting her stylish bob, and this is probably what qualifies her as being the best advice giver.

Nicola is one of Erin's Godmothers, I'm hoping when Erin is an adult, Nicola will be able to offer her words of wisdom and also help her to pack sensibly for the adventures my crazy little Erin will no doubt take.

Samantha – this role goes to Stella. I would like to point out early on, that Stella is not a bed-hopping sex addict, not that I know of! But just like Samantha she is the friend I know I can always say absolutely anything too and she won't be shocked.

That's not to say that my other friends are judgmental in any way, they aren't. But sometimes I have thoughts in my head that I feel shouldn't be there and I can always get them out by telling Stella. Also, much like Samantha, Stella very much has her own life and isn't afraid of that. We see her when we see her and that's ok, but we know she loves us and is there for us whenever we need her.

Despite being the oldest of the gang, and the fact she is most comfortable at home on her mini farm of rescued animals, every time Stella turns up to an event, she glides in all glamour and style, wearing 4-inch heels turning heads as she goes. Stella is not a Godmother to any of my children, but my eldest

Saoirse has asked her to her Confirmation Sponsor, which in my mind is just like choosing your own Godmother.

Miranda – well that obviously only leaves me to complete the fab foursome. Miranda fits me well because, as-well as studying law at college, I am neurotic and constantly whinging about my weight whilst shovelling cake into my mouth.

On the plus side, just like Miranda I care deeply about all of my friends and I am married to a man who loves me with all of his heart. A man who too, has a cool surname that would make a great first name for our future grandchildren (yes, I do think about that kind of thing).

The Extras

Just like any good sit-com, there are always lots of other characters that put in an appearance. I'm going to attempt to cover a few of those that are in my own personal show.

The Old Friends

As in I've known them for a long time, not that they are old. But as we are all now safely 'in' our forties, I guess we are getting old too. Lindsay and Sam are my two closest friends from college. They weren't on the same course as me, but I met Lindsay when I worked in Tokyo Jo's nightclub.

I wasn't keen on Lindsay when I first met her. Although she had only started the day before me, she was very good at telling me what to do, and I thought she was very bossy. She still is very bossy, but it's a trait I have grown to love. Sam was on the same course as Lindsay and I got to know her on nights out.

She's the kind of person you would love to hate, she looks like a cross between Cameron Diaz and Michelle Pfeiffer, she's clever, funny and is good at everything she does, but you just can't help but love Sam, she is gorgeous inside and out, both the ladies are.

They have supported me through break ups, break downs and Lindsay even forgave me when I drove her beloved car into someone else's in the car park at work, because I hadn't driven in years and had obviously forgotten how to do it. As in all good college

156

relationships, they held my hair when puked, danced on tables with me all night and dressed up as a spice girl with me to win the freshers pub crawl when we were in our final year.

I don't see them as often as I'd like, but when I do, the years melt away and we're as close as we've ever been. They just get me, and love me just the way I am. Even when I lost the plot with Lindsay last year for not sending Erin, her Goddaughter, a birthday card. Rather than decide I was too high maintenance and tell me flip off, Lindsay recognised that both she and I hadn't been ourselves of late and that we could both do better. Erin doesn't have a Godfather, but has two Godmothers.

I'd already asked Nicola and as I mulled over a suitable person to take up the role of second Godparent, I just couldn't imagine Lindsay not being in Erin's life in that way. So, two Godmothers it was. She was also my chief bridesmaid, or 'chiefy' as she liked to be called when we bowed. Sam was my other adult bridesmaid, and I always laugh when I think of Sam refusing to swallow communion at the wedding mass as she thought she'd go to hell (she's not catholic). Thanks to Whats App we are now in regular contact and I know we always will be.

The Autism Mummies

When you have a child with special needs, you need a group of friends around you that you can share stories with, much like labour stories with your other mummy friends.

They are your 'tribe', understanding all of the abbreviations like, SLT, ASD, OT, CAMHS, DCA etc. that your other friends would need a translator to decipher. They also understand how tough it is, as despite us all being firmly in the camp of 'different not less', we all fully understand that different is, bloody hard work and at times soul destroying. I have lots of autism mummy friends (and a few dads) and we all get each other through. There is one in particular that I go to most of all, we are very different people, but she is my calming influence when it's all falling apart.

The School Mummies

We all hear stories of competitive mums at the school gates in their SUVs and designer clothes, that doesn't really happen in Leitrim, or if it does then, I've lost the will to notice or give a damn. There are a few of the Mummies that I have struck up

good relationships with over the years and consider to be good friends. We always gravitate towards each other at the play centre, and compare notes on the kids we don't like much, and devise cunning plans on how to steer our own perfect little darlings away from them without turning into helicopter parents. There is one of these Mummies that I'm particularly fond of, you know the one, she makes a mean chocolate biscuit cake!

The Friebours

I live on a lane with about 40 houses, so neighbours can be very far apart. There are lots of really nice people on this lane, but some I am close to and consider friends.

I knew we'd struck gold with our next-door neighbours when on the day we moved in, Tonia knocked on the door with a bottle of whisky – result! She has great taste in whisky and men, I'll never forget the sub-zero December night, when her husband Sean went digging in our front garden with Mick at 11 o-clock at night to find our pipes. They had frozen over and Patrick had ended up in hospital the last time that happened due to swallowing dirty water.

Acts of kindness is what Sean is well known for, but this particular one has always meant the world to me. They also have 3 lovely daughters who have acted as our babysitters and have always been a positive influence in our children's lives. Let's just say the apples didn't fall far from the trees that are their parents. As well as being great neighbours, I am happy to also call them good friends.

Family Friends

With a family as big as Mick's it's impossible to have a close relationship with everyone, but there are a couple of the sister in laws that I get on really well with and always enjoy their company at family events – love you Ciara and Karen.

The Service Providers

That sounds a little bit superior. I certainly don't mean it to, whilst they are people, I pay to go and see, they offer me so much more that nice hair and nails. Maisie always takes longer than she needs when doing my shellac, to let me whine about the bad days I've had since I last saw her. Edel, being a mum of 5 and owner of her own business, has no time for whingers and always gives me a much-needed kick in the arse when I'm sitting in the hairdressing chair feeling sorry for myself, closely followed by a cup of tea and a Twix. She also does a mean blow dry!

The Work Colleagues

We may not socialise outside of work, but are always on hand to bitch together about our bosses, the vendors we use or the photocopier running slow again. Plus, they'll always make the right noises whilst cooing over the new top I bought in Penney's at lunch time.

The Other Good Friends

I'm lucky to have lots of people I get on well with and consider friends. Whilst they aren't in my inner circle, I always enjoy their company. Through work, rest and play I've accumulated many of these friends over the years and I am happy they are in my life.

I really must single out one friend in particular, we only became friends recently when she joined as a leader at the youth club. She really is the kindest person I think I've ever met.

Although she doesn't have children herself, she always seems to grasp exactly what I'm feeling about my own and always offers words of wisdom that hit the spot perfectly.

She is always cooking dinners for other people and giving away the many prizes she wins in competitions.

She is the luckiest person I've ever met. Thank you, Fiona, for the Taylor Swift tickets that gave myself and Saoirse an opportunity to make some magical memories, whilst 'shaking off' our woes.

Back in the sit-com of my life. All of these characters are what make every episode flow so well. Especially at the times when it's more drama than comedy. I am a big believer in talking through life's challenges and like a good bra, professional therapy is very expensive and if you don't get the right fit, it's a waste of money.

So, I am a huge advocate of 'friend therapy' it has sustained me more than adequately over the years, in between the professional sessions I have engaged in. We all can make a difference in people's lives, big or small, every little helps!

To all of my friends.

Thank You.

The Bank of Mum and Dad

It would be remiss of me not to mention our parents when talking about the huge supports we have in our lives. Plus, if I didn't, there's no chance my Dad would ever pick me up from the pub again!

My parents are bloody brilliant. I am not going to pretend we have always had the perfect relationship, we haven't. Nor do we never bicker or drive one another crazy most days, we do. But I can honestly say, Mick and I could not have got through the last few years without them.

In 2015, literally 12 hours after my Dad retired, they were on a ferry heading over with all of their belongs, to start a new life in Ireland. I am only child and they wanted to spend their retirement watching their Grandchildren growing up, so you may say it was an easy move, but I know it wasn't and I couldn't appreciate them more for doing it, even if I don't say it often enough.

Of course, at the age of 43 I'd like to say I never ask them for a loan, but of course do. I think parents never stop dishing out cash. Even if it's not cash, I never leave their house without something, one of my Mum's handbags, biscuits, my car washed.

But it's not their bank of goods I am referring to. It's their bank of goodness. They are here for us financial, practical, emotional and any other 'al' that ever might come up. When I was working, they took care of the children, three afternoons a week, so I wouldn't have to pay over all my wages to a creche. They would feed them, wash them, clothe them usually out of M&S as my Mum has great taste and a loyalty card.

Even though I am no longer working as I am taking Carers Leave, with the raft of appointments I need to attend every week, they still take one or all of the kids at least three afternoons out of seven. Always being on hand to collect Patrick early from school on the days he isn't coping, if I can't there. On the day he recently, tried to climb over a wall to abscond from school, I was in the middle of getting my roots done, and just couldn't leave to collect him, so my Dad did.

Most importantly though they love them all, just the way they are and they look after them, when they know we just don't have the energy do it anymore. Many times, if Mick isn't here, I have had to call my Dad to come and collect the girls to get them out of the house if Patrick's meltdowns get too out of control. He drops them to my Mum and then comes straight back to stand in front of whatever weapon Patrick may be wielding at the time.

One of the most important things they do for us, is let us have time to ourselves. A truly vital part of mine and Mick's life is to have time away from the kids. Caring for Patrick's additional needs, whilst also managing Saoirse and Erin's typical ones, takes its toll and sometimes we just NEED a break.

Once a year, Mick and I pack up and head away somewhere for a few days. It is quite literally the one way our family and our marriage can survive. No battery can go on for ever, and sometimes just an overnight charge isn't quite enough. So, we relish our trip away wherever it may be. Knowing that our charges, human and furry, are in safe hands means we can do it without endless worry or guilt.

Although when we are away, all we do is talk about the children and look for suitable presents to bring back for them. They say friends are the family you pick for yourself. I believe that is true, but I'd also pick exactly the same parents again if ever they come up for re-selection.

Last but not least, I must mention my Mother-in-Law, Kathleen. Although she doesn't live beside us, nor is in good enough health to mind the kids anymore. She is the root of the strength in our family. Despite, not have been expected to live very long when she was born, she is now in her seventy fourth year and will probably outlive us all.

At the age of 37, she was widowed with just six-weeks' notice, and reared 8 children between the ages of 2 and 15 by herself.

I have no doubt a lot of Mick's strength came from watching his Mam; just getting on with it.' I will always have a huge amount of respect for her and although, Mick isn't the gushy type, I know he would be lost without her.

Independent Woman

This year, would have seen the 100th birthday of my beloved, Nana Holywell and her twin sister Auntie Nellie. Both of the women were huge influences in my life and play a significant role in the fondest of my childhood memories.

Although moving, to the small Welsh town of Holywell (hence her name), she missed home and I spent many a happy school holidays visiting my Nana's native Leicester, where we stayed with Auntie Nellie and Uncle Cliff.

I loved their house, except for the outside bathroom. It was here I learnt to squat when you pee, rather than sit down and risk freezer burns on my delicate little bum! Auntie Nellie married later in life, and did not have children, so whenever I went there, I was spoiled rotten.

I would be allowed to stay up late playing Chase the Ace, for pennies around the fancy dark wood dining table, I was allowed to place bets on the horses with my Uncle Cliff, I was taken to every park across the city of Leicester, my favourite being taken every year to the Abbey Park Show. One year, Even making the front cover of the Leicester Mercury newspaper pictured feeding a goose!

My Auntie Nellie was always well presented, I used to play with her powder puff, old fashioned hairbrush and would smear her rouge on my cheeks whilst sitting at her fancy dressing table. I still catch my breath when I get the smell of traditional beauty products at the make-up counter, thinking of her. In her later years she never answered the door without a full face of make-up, with extra red lipstick. It reflected her bold character and sense of mischief! I don't have a single photograph of her where she wasn't smiling or laughing.

I remember visiting once, when she was heading towards her 90th year, and she took great delight in making my Dad blush, telling him about a TV program she had recently watched about how penis extensions were the next big thing, literally!!

Not many people can leave my Dad with nothing to say. She was always able to find humour in everything. I feel I have inherited my wit from her and finding the light moments in the darkest of days has been an absolute lifesaver for me in recent years.

The Midlands, was not the only exotic destination Nana took me to. It was as her travel companion to Australia to visit her daughter Linda, when I was just 9, was what firmly injected the magic wanderlust in my blood.

Due to a Quantas strike, we got to spend 4 days in Singapore on the journey home, which meant, as well as enjoying the pleasures of the land down under, I got to experience an exotic new world, filled with an excitement I'd never thought possible (Scarborough didn't quite cut it as a holiday destination after that!) As an adult, I accompanied her to Australia again, to attend my cousin Leanne's wedding. I spent 2 of my 3 weeks there, visiting friends in Sydney and expanding my love of new cultures, and new beers.

When I was 20, my wanderlust and desire for new adventures took me to California to work as Wrangler at a summer camp. I was so proud of myself to do it all alone, I was a truly independent woman.

I embarked on this particular adventure knowing absolutely no-one. It was a decision I thought I would live to regret on the first leg of my journey, when at 3am I boarded a National Express bus in Preston (near Manchester) bound for Heathrow. It was filled to the rafters with very drunk Glaswegians, determined to sing rebel songs the whole way to London. To say I was uncomfortable is a little understated, nowadays I'd probably just join in the singing, but 43 is very different to 20. When I got to the airport, I spotted lots of gangs of people with the same 'Camp-Counsellors-USA' luggage tag as me, all grouped together having the craic.

I was so tempted to join them, but instead I sat nervously, pretending to read my book. It was only after I realised, that I hadn't turned a page in 20 minutes and the book was in fact, upside down, that I decided to make the move and introduce myself to one of the groups. I never looked back! This was my summer of discovery. Riding horses through the forests of the Southern California mountains, making a gaggle of international friends, sampling exciting new foods, and most memorably, meeting wonderful children with terminal illnesses, that showed me the true meaning of living life to the full.

I even got to ride on the back of a quad bike with a

Calvin Klein model and played pool at the local bar, with Chandler from Friends - I kid you not!! The summer of 1996 was the best of my young life, and apologies for the cliché, but it was 'the making of me'.

Had my Nana not brought me here, there and everywhere from Bagillt to Brisbane, I don't think I ever would have had the confidence or the desire to make that trip.

That love of new adventures and travel is what made me bite the bullet and move to Ireland. I came here on a 2-year contract, that was in 2002! Here we go with the biggest cliché of them all – I met Mick and the rest is history. My Nana helped to make me an Independent woman. Just like she was. Being widowed at 60, with 3 of her 4 children living abroad, before Ryanair was even a twinkle in Michael O'Leary's eye, way before straight forward, cheap travel was an option.

But this blue rinsed, little old lady, with a passion for chocolate eclairs, made the most of the life she had and embraced it with all of her might. You didn't know these wonderful women, but you will recognise them.

We all have wonderful, strong women like this in our lives. Women that shaped who we are, who blazed a trail that we need to keep on burning.

In September, we held a mass in their honour, celebrating their memory. Even as a staunch agnostic, and dedicated Darwinist. My Mum wanted to mark their memory appropriately. My Autistic Son, Patrick doesn't 'do' church. Every visit, it has gotten harder and harder, from rolling around on the floor, to refusing to participate in any way, even at the lovely monthly children's service that is offered locally in Mohill.

He and Erin go to a Church of Ireland School, but we are all Catholic, so he has tried both flavours and finds neither to his taste. At Saoirse's enrolment mass for Confirmation last year, Patrick sat in the row banging his head off the pew in front of him, shouting "this is fucking stupid, I want to leave." Mick and I decided that was probably the time to stop taking Patrick to mass!

My Mum didn't mind that he wouldn't be going today, to be honest I think she shares his sentiments on religion! I however had hoped that he may come for a little while, my good friend Nicola has always been on hand to remove all or any my children, should they become difficult, at important masses. I was hoping she might oblige today, so I could have Mick by my side, rather than at home minding Patrick.

We tried for weeks, but there was no convincing Patrick, then Halleluiah, he said that morning, he would come for a few minutes and was willing to sit quietly at the back with Mick, leaving if he felt uncomfortable. But this is my life, and nothing is ever straight forward. My 6-year-old daughter, Erin, decided now was the time to have an epic meltdown about what clothes she would or would not wear. Even when we finally agreed to let her wear her filthy, ripped, too small LOL leggings, she had passed the point of no return. There would be no convincing her that anything other than rolling about on

169

her bed screaming hysterically was an option.

Erin has serious meltdowns, so much so she has also been assessed for the possibility of being Autistic too. She apparently isn't, but that message hasn't reached the meltdown part of her brain, so it continues to launch meltdowns that would measure on the Richter Scale. Sadly, due to the challenging behaviour, of Patrick at home, Erin experiences trauma and this drives her own challenging behaviour.

Not to be out done by her big brother, Erin's meltdowns, usually start, just as one of Patrick's finishes. Never a dull moment in our house! Luckily Saoirse had been at a sleepover the previous night, and was meeting us at the church, so we didn't have any teenage terror thrown into the mix. So, with 5 minutes to spare before mass started and knowing my Dad's watch was set precisely to 3 different time zones, I had to leave.

I had hoped to attend this mass with my family, it was so important to me to commemorate this special day. I walked up to the mass by myself, but I didn't feel like an independent woman. I just felt Alone.

That feeling of being alone is something no one warned me about when you are a parent to a child with special needs. You are surrounded by professionals of every shape, size and support agency. My parents moved here to support us. I engage in friend therapy (basically me whinging, whilst eating cake) regularly, and I am blessed to be have a supportive, engaged, husband.

But often, I do feel so very alone.

Logistically, I am regularly, physically alone, in order to facilitate the right environment to make life easier for Patrick, I attend things without Mick as he has to stay home taking my place, as carer. I sit alone most days, in the waiting room of the endless appointments.

But it's more than that. Alone with my thoughts, alone with my fears, alone with my emotions and worst of all alone dealing with the fact that, I don't always feel the way I'm apparently 'supposed' to feel about being a Special Needs Mum and at times it's really bloody scary.

But then, I suppose that is the same for everyone. No matter what is going on in our lives, there are so many things we aren't 'supposed' to talk about or aren't even 'supposed' to feel, but I believe maybe it's time we all bloody started talking about what we really do feel.

That is why I wrote this book, sharing the way we really feel, recognising that it isn't wrong, will hopefully help us all. Not feeling guilt or shame, for not adhering to an emotional rule book, that was written by someone who hasn't shared in the same experiences as each of us.

Our experiences aren't always unique, but the way we feel about them belongs to us as individuals. We each have a right to our own personal emotions, without being made to feel they are wrong because someone writes a magazine article deciding they are bad. Or worse, someone with a PHD in 'something we've never heard of', decides to write a book on their 'research'. No one but you, has a PHD in you!

If we all take a leap of faith in ourselves, truly being honest with each other, then maybe we can be honest with ourselves.

That, isn't such a lonely place after all.

It's a liberating one!

Who knows just might all, end up living healthily ever after!

Epilogue

If I had a penny for the number of times a day I say, "I give up!" I would be a very rich woman, I think we all would be!

We give up with the wonky WIFI, the remote (out of) control, the kids homework that is fit for a Harvard Professor. We all regularly reach these points in the day, when we have just absolutely had enough of whatever it is that has driven us crazy in that moment.

But this year, which has probably been the worst of my life if I am truly honest, there have been many days where I have almost totally given up.

I have regularly taken to my bed for a nap, I just want to sleep so I can escape everything that is actually going on, and the weight I feel in my head and heart.

I have given up communicating in so many ways, lost in my phone, hiding from the real world, trying to fix problems that aren't mine, in the hope, I will feel something positive from doing that. Worst of all, everything around me, has made me feel so angry and bitter. I have looked for the bad in everything, where I used to see the good.

At times I have wanted to give up completely, whatever that may look like.

So, as 2020 looms (or has passed when you read this), and we all make the decisions to make ourselves healthier, more productive and happier by resolving to give up the things that are dragging us down.

I am only giving up one thing, I'm giving up, giving up. Because this year has taught me, that no matter how bad it gets, I, we, can do this. Nobody ever said life was easy, but it is worth it.

Oh, and diet coke, I'm also giving up diet coke, because that is really bad for me too.

I hope 2020 brings you many happy endings and if it doesn't, then you never know what will happen in the next chapter, so keep reading x.

With Warm Wishes

Faye x

And Finally...

A few years ago, I read a horror story that sadly wasn't fiction.

It was the story of the Naughton Family in my neighbouring county of Roscommon. Paula and Padraic have 3 gorgeous sons, Archie aged 13 and Twins George and Isaac aged 9. All 3 boys have been diagnosed with Duchenne Muscular Dystrophy. A muscle wasting disease with an average life expectancy of late teens to early twenties.

All three boys are now wheelchair users.

Refusing to let their sons' diagnoses end their lives right there and then, Paula and Padraic adopted the mottos to #KeepMoving to #KeepMarching to #NeverEVERGiveUp and to somehow maintain #Hope.

Their story is what gets me up out of bed on the days that I feel my life is crumbling and that I just want to hide away.

Because, if they can do it – we all can!

Like so many of us, on hearing their story, I decided that I just had to do something, I didn't know what, but just something to offer my support.

I am currently' working with the boys', Mum, one of my heroes, Paula Kerr and she has agreed to work with me on writing a series of books, to

1. Educate and Change people's attitudes to Disabilities and

2. To raise funds toward medical care and supporting

the housing and changing care needs of Archie, George and Isaac in the coming years.

So, where do YOU come in?

I really want to hear from you, to tell your stories, to be included in the books/blog.

This is your chance to make a positive difference.

I'll be upfront about this, you will NOT be paid for your contribution to this book, but neither will I.

ALL PROFITS from these books will go directly to the JOIN OUR BOYS TRUST……. you can find out more information and make a donation, if you would like on www.joinourboys.org

So, what do YOU do next……..?

Paula and I are hoping to work on a series of fundraising books, for general release in 2020.

first book will focus on the real-life stories of young people with disabilities or additional needs. Not just the story of their condition, but the story of them: their life, their hopes, dreams, fears, passions and pet hates.

We aim to give a voice to young people who are so much more than their condition alone, because focusing solely on this disables them even more.

Please send your details through one of the following channels and we will send you more information of how you can get involved.

✉ - fayehayden8110@gmail.com

⌨ - via Bedtime Stories for Mothers and Others on

Facebook and Twitter

🖱 - On my website www.fayehayden.life

Then please like and share "Join Our Boys Trust" on Facebook and buy a book or three when they go on sale in 2020

THANK YOU

Printed in Poland
by Amazon Fulfillment
Poland Sp. z o.o., Wrocław

53537180R00107